Label with Care

A behaviour management book for parents

by Teresa Bliss

Illustrated by Frances Vesma

Published by Lucky Duck Publishing Ltd
3 Thorndale Mews, Clifton, Bristol
BS8 2HX, UK

Designed by Barbara Maines
Printed in the UK by The Book Factory, Mildway Avenue, London N1 4RS

© Teresa Bliss 1998
Reprinted April 2000, February 2002

All rights reserved. No part of this publication may be reproduced, stored in a retrieval system, or transmitted in any form or by any means, electronic, mechanical, photocopying, recording or otherwise, without the prior, written permission of the publisher.

The right of the author to be identified as author of this work has been asserted by him in accordance with the Copyright, Design and Patents Act, 1988.

Materials may be photocopied within the purchasing institution if applicable.

Acknowledgements

It is not possible to write a book such as this in isolation from one's life experiences. I would like to thank some of the people who have been significant in my life and have helped me learn and build on those life experiences.

- My parents, who gave me my first experience of family life and so much to build on.
- My brothers whose love and friendship continues to be an important part of my life.
- Heather who first encouraged me and gave me the confidence of a professional self.
- Natalie who helped to continue that process with her belief in my abilities.
- Mary who facilitated the writing of my first book.
- Barbara and George who said they would like to publish it.
- My greatest thanks go to Steve and our children: Steve for his love, emotional and practical support, Chloe, Oliver and Eleanore for the contribution they have made to this book and for being the wonderful people they are.

**This book is dedicated to Steve,
Chloe, Oliver and Eleanore with all my love.**

Contents

Introduction		5

Part One

Chapter 1	Parenting Styles and Cultural Influences	8
Chapter 2	Meeting Needs	20
Chapter 3	Self-Concept	28
Chapter 4	Sibling Rivalry	36
Chapter 5	Difficulties for Parents	42
Chapter 6	Rules and Values	49

Part Two

Chapter 7	Bad Behaviour	57
Chapter 8	Discipline and Punishment	64
Chapter 9	Smacking	77
Chapter 10	Serious Misbehaviour	83
Chapter 11	Bad Language	94
Chapter 12	Spoiling	98

Part Three

Chapter 13	Encouraging Independence	106
Chapter 14	Praise and Rewards	114
Chapter 15	Listening	119

Appendices

Appendix 1	Autism	127
Appendix 2	Hyperactivity	128
Bibliography		131

Introduction

This book is intended to help and guide parents through the difficult years of bringing up children. It focuses on children's behaviour and family relationships.

The cliché that this is the only job for which there is no training is so true! It is a job we may legitimately start at 16 years of age when we are still developing and growing. For most of us it is the most important job we will perform in society - that of rearing the next generation. The current debate about what parents should and should not do is confusing and largely unhelpful. It is often discussed by male politicians who probably have, or had, only a passing acquaintance with their own offspring in their early years. Bringing up children is a wonderful and rewarding experience; it is also unremittingly hard work.

The style and arrangement of the book is intended to help parents think about their own beliefs and practices for bringing up children. At the beginning of each chapter is a questionnaire that asks you to think about your beliefs on the topic covered in that chapter and to critically examine them. Families go on repeating the same patterns, making the same mistakes, without really knowing why until someone gains an insight into the dynamics of the family. Then positive changes can be made. Conflict between brothers and sisters is often carried on well into adulthood, making the adult relationships difficult, uneasy, or impossible.

Our children's psychological development is as important as their physical development. As a society we have made great strides throughout this century to improve children's health and their physical environments. However we have paid scant attention to their psychological well-being. I always liken the psyche (the mind and spirit) to a bone. If a leg bone is broken and not properly set then one is likely to walk with a limp and that bone will be crooked. So it is with the psyche. If a person suffers a trauma, if there are unresolved issues and conflict, they will remain within the subconscious and the result will be a psychological limp. I have lost count of the number of adults who do not have a good relationship with grown-up siblings, or who are driven by a need to compete with them. When they stand back and analyse their behaviour it always returns to issues and problems in their own childhood.

Why do so many adults dread family gatherings? It is usually at a time of celebration when brothers and sisters come together. The first hour or so is tolerable, even enjoyable, then the old rivalries and unresolved family issues surface in different guises into the adult world. The adult brothers and sisters pick up on or create problems that have their roots in childhood, where frustrations, resentments and perceived hurts or injustices have lain unresolved, the details of which have been forgotten but the feelings remain. It is these feelings that stay with us and dictate how we will behave.

The Child Within Us

We all have a child within us that is constantly determining how we should respond in our adult lives. That child within us is the child that we were, with the fears, hurts and humiliations as well as the love and encouragement we experienced. Sometimes, we were made angry as children and not allowed to express that anger. The anger, resentment and hurt can remain buried all our lives, but it is still there. Without understanding those feelings, without the memory of what it actually felt like to be a frightened, confused, humiliated child, the pattern is likely to be repeated on the next generation. When I see adults' anger over some relatively trivial event I wonder what is driving such a passionate response. It is likely to be an anger within that adult that is unresolved, and very possibly a rage from the child within.

I hope you will begin to understand a little of what drives your behaviour; you the adult, or your child within you. On your journey through this book I hope you begin to discover the child that is within you and understand how it affects the adult you are now and how it impinges upon your attitudes and abilities as a parent.

Touching

I feel I have to give this a special mention because touching has become a taboo in some circles in our society. I believe that touching, stroking and hugging are essential to the psychological well-being of our children. Children need good, positive, physical contact with their parents. It is an essential part of good parenting and it is therefore their right to have it. We all know what is good and what is bad touching. Even the perpetrators of sexual deviance understand the difference and their understanding of their perversion is underscored by their insistence on secrecy and silence. Any harmful touch is totally wrong and should not be experienced by any child in this world. Sadly, some do experience hideous crimes. Those children are in a minority and their experiences must not influence us to stop touching and cuddling our little ones - they need it.

When children are first born the quality of a parent's bonding love is felt through gentle loving looks, cuddles and physical handling. As time goes on the adult hand that lifts up a crying child who is hurt or tired will convey love. The adult lap available for rest, a story, reassurance and so on, help to give a feeling of security, acceptance and self-esteem.

There is no age at which hugs and cuddles should cease for boys or girls. After all, what adult doesn't enjoy the comfort of a partner's hug at the end of a hectic work day? School is a very stressful place for children and physical contact is necessary to most children's well-being. In fact I do believe that more physical contact of the right type described above would help dramatically reduce the teenage pregnancy rate. If they had plenty of cuddles at home then they would not need to seek them elsewhere, with the inevitable turning to sexual exploration. Without exception, all the sexually active teenagers I have worked with have been looking for love - someone to love them, or something to love.

More expressed parental love is needed.

I have come across some very strange attitudes to cuddling and touching children. One of the strangest is that male children should not be positively touched or cuddled because it will ultimately affect their sexuality. This is obviously ridiculous. One of the questions I ask parents who hold this particular attitude is "How did the child get here in the first place?" Grown men and women enjoy physical contact. Although it is usually of a sexual nature, it is not always. All human beings of whatever age need physical contact of the loving sort that comes with positive touching and friendly hugs.

Using The Book

I have tried to offer you a framework for thinking through the early experiences that have made you the person you are today. At the beginning of each section are some questions. They have been formulated to get you thinking about the issue covered in the section. Answer it before you read what I have to say, then answer it again sometime later, once you have given yourself time to digest the information, to see if your ideas have changed. At this point you may find questions that I have not given you. What questions do you need to ask yourself? There are a great many questions about your own childhood. This is deliberate because the child rearing practices we experience as children become our blueprint for the way we, in turn, bring up our own children. Most of us simply repeat the experience of parenting we had as children. If you are trying to make changes then it will be necessary to understand why you are as you are, and do what you do.

When answering the questions give yourself time to reflect on why you have those particular feelings. Think back, can you remember what generated those feelings? This will help you understand what drives you and dictates the way you behave. With greater self knowledge you will be better able to leave behind strategies that are unproductive within your family and replace them with new ones. Which new ones will be up to you to choose because all families are as different as the individuals within them. I realise that by reading this you are trying to add to your parenting skills and there are no easy answers. In writing this book I have drawn on my own experience with my three children, and over twenty years of working with parents and teaching other people's children. I have also used the research of others and provide a book list at the end if you wish to take your reading further.

I have used the term parent throughout, it is meant to be the person who is primarily responsible for the day-to-day management of the child. A more accurate term could be significant caretaker, but that is clumsy. I am very aware that there are many variables on what constitutes a family and that children live with people other than their biological parents. They can form attachments to those people that are just as strong as the loving bonds between children and their natural parents. Dealing with children on a day-to-day basis, regardless of whether they are our own or not, will require us to look to that original blueprint that was developed when we were children ourselves.

Parents' Questions

Chapter 1 - Parenting Styles And Cultural Influences

Ask yourself:

1. What do you believe your parenting style to be?

2. If your children are old enough, ask them to read through the lists on pages 9 and 10 and place you as an authoritarian, democratic or permissive parent.

3. What would you say your partner's style is?

4. What was your parents' style?

5. How has society changed since you were a child?

6. Have you consciously changed your parenting style away from the way you were raised?

7. What have you retained of your parents' management style?

8. How do you see societal or cultural influences in your life?

Parenting Styles and Cultural Influences

To hear many parents talk to and about their children it would be easy to believe that there was only one style of parenting possible - the authoritarian style. Yet in their dealings with adults they show a variety of personality styles.

Below I have outlined three types of parenting. I have called them:

The *authoritarian style*, with rigid boundaries, where parents behave like dictators.

The *democratic style,* where parents allow opportunities for children to make choices and decisions for themselves in ways that are safe and suitable for them.

The *permissive style,* where there are no proper boundaries and everything tends to be externalised and becomes everyone else's fault.

The lists contain some of the features that make up the three different parenting styles. Some parents will have all the features of one particular style, however the majority of parents will have a large number of the characteristics of one and some of the other two. Most of us can be all three within the space of an hour. When I showed this book to my two eldest children they decided I was basically a democratic parent but I could be a bit of the others at different times. Interestingly, one felt I was mainly democratic/authoritarian, the other thought my mix was democratic/permissive.

This raised in my mind all sorts of questions about why they reacted as they did. For example, was it indicative of how I treat them? Am I more lenient with one child than another? My son felt I was inclined towards the permissive, whereas my daughter felt my inclination was towards the autocratic. Is this a cultural/gender bias, or was it simply how they were feeling about me at the time? Did they say different things simply because they didn't want to have the same answer as each other? Or did it reflect their personalities?

The Authoritarian Style Parent
* Believes in discipline coming from him/her.
* Is strict.
* Has a distant relationship.
* Tells children off without protecting their self-esteem.
* Has strict rules.
* Does things for the child's sake or own good.
* Takes all decisions for children.
* Believes in compliant children who obey immediately.
* Criticises, labels and calls the child names.
* Does not listen very often.

* Insists that his/her needs are met without due regard to the children's needs.
* Believes he/she must always win.
* Gives advice unasked.
* Sibling rivalry will be high, early bonding could be very good or very bad.

The Democratic Style Parent
* Believes that all family members should have a say in making rules.
* Listens.
* Believes in everyone winning and having his or her needs met.
* Has a close relationship with children.
* Negotiates with children and helps them to make their own decisions in an informed way.
* Uses constructive criticism and gives informational feedback to child.
* Uses encouragement and discussion to guide children.
* Regards behaviour of young children as a sharing of responsibility.
* Only gives advice when asked.
* Sibling rivalry will be low with good bonding.

The Permissive Style Parent
* Has no apparent restrictions or limits.
* Is frequently indolent and gives in.
* Is often bewildered because the children are out of control.
* Frequently asks questions such as "what can you do with them these days?".
* Allows their children to hold power and bully them.
* Makes no attempt to be assertive.
* Does not have his/her own needs met.
* Always loses or gives in.
* Allows children to make all the decisions.
* Sibling bonding will be poor and rivalry high.

The Authoritarian Style of Parenting

These parents do make life very hard for themselves. They believe in firmly imposed discipline, they have rules, and expect compliant children who obey immediately. They are loving parents. It is how they believe they should show their love that causes the problems. They believe in maintaining a certain distance in order to preserve their position of authority.

When children are very small it is usually easy to be an authoritarian parent. Children will obey strict rules because they know nothing else. Being totally dependent on their parents for basic survival needs such as food, clothes and shelter, and having the inborn capacity for unconditional love, children will believe it when parents tell them the restrictive or hurtful things they are doing to them is "for their own good". Some children will totally absorb their parents' values. They will accept the tough discipline and in adulthood they will behave similarly. At school and in wider society they are likely to be seen as children who are obedient and easy to handle because they are compliant within an authoritarian structure. It will suit their personality to assimilate such attitudes and values. They will think like their parents and are unlikely to give their parents cause for concern as they go through their teenage years.

It is when children are not so accepting of such methods and behaviour that problems, particularly in the teenage years, arise. All will go well until the children are able to compare other families with their own. They will meet children at school who will give them insights into other ways of behaving that may seem more attractive. Television will also impart clear messages about family life. As children start to think for themselves and begin to determine what behaviours and values are for them, so the external influences are used as comparisons.

Children who reject authoritarian parenting will resent unnecessary rules, the heavy discipline, and the parents' apparent selfishness in always demanding that they win and their needs are met. As they grow older, the children will not listen to advice. These children are likely to be rebellious, angry young people, all the more difficult because they have not learned to take decisions and exercise their rights in informed and responsible ways. They will have identified with their authoritarian parents and become authoritarian themselves. Alternatively, they may be unable to stand up for themselves in any way and be far too acquiescent.

Both groups have a high probability for getting into trouble as teenagers. The reasons can be complex but there are two main ones. The first because they will be learning to flex their muscles and use their own power for the first time. The second because they are likely to be malleable. They will be led astray because they will allow more dominant characters to tell them what to do.

Many parents give up being authoritarian as their children grow and resist the rules. They realise they cannot get away with using such power tactics and maintain a close loving relationship with their children. The problem for them comes when deciding what to replace their authoritarian tactics with, when for years they have taken the stance that the child MUST do as it is told. They have always taken a win-lose stance: I the parent must win, you the child must lose. When they have believed that they must always win, they have been looking at a very complex relationship with tunnel vision. In abandoning their authoritarian practices they become permissive parents in the face of opposition from their children and in the absence of knowing what else to do. The problem is that they see their relationship with their children in polarised terms.

Parents who decide that they can no longer use the powerful authoritarian way, frequently then adopt the practices of permissive parents. They stop trying to enforce any boundaries, and have none. They become bewildered' and distressed by their children's cheek, thoughtlessness and uncontrollable behaviour.

The Permissive Style of Parenting

It seems to me that parents who are naturally permissive in an indolent way are few and far between. Permissiveness is often the other side of the authoritarian coin. Permissive parents also love their children, but again it is the way they love them that causes the problems.

Parents who are always permissive are likely to have children who bully and push them around. These children will be demanding and appear spoilt. The children will be critical and always dissatisfied (see the chapter on Spoiling).

The permissive parent may well hold all the beliefs and values of an authoritarian parent, but not have the ability to enforce their will on their child due to a number of reasons such as lack of stamina, poor self-image, fear of exerting or using power, or an inability to confront issues and problems.

On the other hand, the permissive parent may, in fact, hold none of the beliefs and values of the authoritarian parent. They may have taken to extremes the view that children should be able to explore for themselves, find their own identities and make their own decisions about how to behave. These parents abdicate from their responsibilities, which results in them failing to give clear guidance and a firm structure to their children's lives. The children end up taking control at too early an age from necessity, not because they want to. The children appear brash, demanding, spoilt, rude and even out of control. They are unhappy individuals who find it difficult to accept adults' authority, yet yearn for the security it would give them. However, what they need most is the security of clear and firm boundaries from their parents. When relationships have deteriorated to such a problematic level then outside professional help is usually needed. This is partly because those involved cannot see how things have gone so badly wrong, and also because both parents and child require help to establish what will become a new regime. An outsider will be able to facilitate in organising and initiating new dynamics to bring about a new order within the family (see Part Three).

A professional working with a permissive parent would be helping them to be assertive and consistent, and to introduce a measure of control into the child's life; to take decisions and set limits, and stick to them; to ensure that the needs of all family members, including parents, are met. Parents have a duty to take a degree of responsibility for their children; one of their greatest duties is to help their children to lead emotionally balanced and secure lives. Children who make all the decisions are very rarely balanced and emotionally stable; they are frightened and angry. It does mean that parents have to occasionally say "no," and mean it. Parents who have been permissive and are trying to establish control will not only find saying "no" hard, but sticking with it will be even more difficult. They are likely to face a whole range of behaviours from their child who will be trying to coax, bully or intimidate them into reverting to permissiveness. It will be a bumpy road but well worth the effort in the end.

The Democratic Style of Parenting

The democratic parent will not see their relationship in power terms. They will want to ensure that their children are able to regulate their own behaviour without an adult always present. They will encourage their children to manage their own behaviour rather than always having it managed for them. They will expect that their children will take responsibility for their own behaviour.

They will respect their children's rights and position within the family, and try to ensure that all family members have their needs met. This will be achieved by negotiation and through trying to accommodate everyone, with each family member's requirements being treated with respect. They will solve problems that arise together. Children will be asked their opinions and given genuine choices. Democratic parents listen to their children with genuine respect and concern for their views. Communication is good. Both parents and children regularly talk to one another. When criticism is needed it will be given in a positive and constructive framework, giving children information about their behaviour with help to avoid the situation next time and ideas for improving or altering social skills. No negative labelling or name-calling occurs.

Democratic parents do have to say "no" sometimes. While they encourage their children to make choices and take decisions for themselves, sometimes it is appropriate for the parents to take charge. They explain and discuss the reasons for their decisions, but if they have to be firm and take an unpopular decision then it is not something the democratic parent will refuse to do. They know that the ultimate responsibility is theirs, and their first duty is for the well being of their children. It becomes a finely crafted balancing act that few get right all the time.

These parents have a warm and close relationship with their children. The family will, for the most part, enjoy life together and value time together. Sibling rivalry will be present but less so than in families with the other two parenting styles. Democratic parents are the most likely to have good relationships with their children as they grow into adults.

Power, Influence and Age

Once you give birth to your baby it is likely that you will be a parent all of your remaining years. Being a parent to a child of seven will require different skills to those used with a child of seventeen or twenty-seven. But how different? Your opportunity to use physical power over your child is very short-lived. Parents who most frequently resort to physical domination in the early years, and do not develop other skills in handling their child, find themselves without useful ways of coping by the time their children are young teenagers. As already noted they are also likely to have resentful, rebellious youngsters who have a very difficult time in their teens.

You may be able to control your child with financial penalties, emotional blackmail, loss of privileges and so on, but again, these controls only have a limited useful life. If you still need to impose heavy, frequent controls by the time your child is nine or ten then you are likely to be heading for trouble. I discuss this at length later. To be an effective parent throughout the troublesome teens you need to be able to genuinely influence your children. This means developing the skills of a democratic parent as early as possible so that you are well practised by the time power is unusable. The consistent democratic parent is likely to have the best relationships and will certainly have more influence.

Cultural Influences

There are influences that affect our lives with a subtlety that make them almost invisible to us. The notion of an individual has to be seen within the context of a society that has also been shaped by many influences.

Individual families do not operate in a vacuum. Everyone has pictures of who they are within society and this, to a certain extent, influences how they act and behave. Even a rebellious stance is shaped by the very culture that is being rejected. There is a social influence on everyone's behaviour and that is set within a wider cultural and historical context.

If we look back to Victorian England, we can see its rigid manners and hierarchical social structure enabled everyone to "know their place" within society. Emotions were not expressed publicly, if at all. Husbands and wives referred to each other as Mr or Mrs when talking with acquaintances. Wives had almost total responsibility for childrearing. Move on to the "swinging sixties" and the influence of the longhaired hippie generation, and to the nineties where it is now customary to call adults by their first names regardless of status. Men expect to be involved in their children's upbringing, and emotions are not only allowed to be expressed but actively encouraged. It has been understood that suppression of emotions can damage mental health. The contrast between British culture of the 19th century and that of the end of the 20th century is indeed great.

Furthermore, there are a great many people from very different cultures living in Britain now. Children with parents who grew up in other parts of the world will be getting very different messages about behaviour from those who have lived in this country all their lives. As an example, in the Asian community humility is a quality to be admired, especially in women. Deference to elders and control of emotion is generally encouraged to a greater extent than in the native British population.

The values and standards of society as a whole are reflected in the different expectations parents and children have, resulting in changes in behavioural patterns for individuals. Many practices today would have been considered totally unacceptable or sheer bad manners a few years ago. An example of a social role now in confusion is that many women object to men holding doors open for them, some men do not consider that they ought to hold doors open for women, and are sometimes considered rude, particularly by older women. This is an area where many men consider they are in a no-win situation - in many ways it typifies the confusion we are now in.

More seriously, young women expect to have careers and children, and they expect their husbands to do their fair share of child rearing. This will inevitably have an effect on working patterns and employment practices because for too long the world of work has behaved as though the adults employed were single with no family responsibilities. This has mitigated men from their duties as fathers and meant an imbalance in child rearing, with women taking too large a role. Many fathers have, in the past, been virtual strangers to their children, resulting in deep regrets on both sides. In recent years young men are beginning to demand the opportunity to take a more active role in their children's lives. This is beginning to bring about a cultural change within our society.

The reasons for this change in attitude are many and complex. One, of course, is the pill. Safer, more reliable contraception has enabled women to delay and control when they have babies. This has enabled them to have a more equal relationship with their husbands. Women are as well educated, able to earn as much money as their partners, if not more, and expect to have a relationship of equality with husbands who regard them as partners rather than chattels or servants. This cultural change is well underway and the dynamics of married relationships are very different from those I witnessed in my childhood.

This all has an impact on how adult humans raise their young. Many children are growing up with very different perspectives on how relationships between men and women are conducted. Their expectations about themselves and how they should behave have changed dramatically since their grandparents' times. It is not to say life is worse, or that standards of behaviour have slipped, because they have not. Bad behaviour among young children is still unusual enough to be noteworthy.

In 1989 a report was published entitled Discipline in Schools. It had been commissioned by the Government and chaired by Lord Elton to look at standards of behaviour in schools, partly because there is a myth engendered by the press that discipline has become poor and children unruly. No evidence for this could be found. In fact, during the work of the Elton commission, its Vice Chair, Dr R. Bennett, spoke to a group of elderly villagers to find out their views on behaviour at school by comparison with today. They repeated the timeless view that young people are generally out of control and badly behaved. He gave them some examples of bad behaviour to which they tut-tutted about youngsters of today and said how his examples obviously confirmed their views - until he pointed out that his examples in fact came from the records of the village school they themselves had attended. To their credit they were embarrassed, and then remembered and recounted their misdemeanours. Historically, literature is peppered with complaints from adults that standards are declining and children's behaviour is beyond reasonable control. It is a complaint that is as old as human society itself.

I do not hold with the view that there has been a decline in moral values. I would ask what is meant by moral values? From where are the values derived? Whom do they benefit? Values have changed - hypocrisy is more likely to be exposed.

Governments have an influence on the values of society, and throughout the 1980s and early 1990s British society was encouraged to be materialistic in a selfish way. We were told to "understand a little less and condemn a little more" - unless it was one of their number being investigated for corruption, cheating, or fathering children outside a stable relationship. Government, in recent years, set a very low moral standard. They have made life harder for those with less money and easier for those with more, through legislation that has greatly increased the wealth of a few and increased the burden of many. This has worked against children. Given the years of hypocrisy amongst this country's leadership, is it any wonder that there is confusion within the general population about moral standards? Parents have to work within the context of society; when government leadership has so much difficulty within its own ranks deciding between right and wrong, why should we be surprised that some parents are experiencing unusually challenging behaviour from their children? For so long government said "don't do as we do, but do as we say" - wise parents know that a good role model is vital and words of that nature are wasted. Society is, at the moment, lacking in a compassionate, truthful, and honest role model, but historically, when were politicians able to give us such a role model? People sought it in another institution that again kept to the faith of "do as we say" whilst often hiding what they did.

Religion

In this country religion no longer plays the part it once did in our society. Some people say it is because the church has lost its influence that moral standards have declined. Looking round the world I find it hard to accept. Northern Ireland with the Protestant and Catholic divisions and resulting brutality; Iran with the religious fundamentalists brutally persecuting those who disagree; Catholicism has its seat in Italy and is regarded as a Catholic country, how then does it account for the Mafia? I could continue with examples across the world, such as the treatment of street children in Catholic Latin American countries. Religion does not make for safe, emotionally stable societies, but people do. The way they are nurtured and loved when young is what is important. During Victorian times, religion was held in high esteem. Prostitution, drunkenness, slavery, child labour and violence were all rife. We are all much safer on the streets now than we would have been in the "good old days".

Looking back over this chapter on parenting styles, and this discussion of cultural and religious influences, it is easy to see what an enormous task we are faced with in a society that is increasingly complex. It is said that we live in changing times but looking back, when was life ever static? The pace has quickened and the nature of change has altered. In the past society evolved and reacted to external circumstances as necessary. Now we are subjected to technical change that was beyond any foresight a generation ago. Social demography is altering in an unforeseen way. The job of managing so many old people who no longer earn money is something society has to learn to cope with. What priority will we give to children's services, such as education, in the new order? What role will grandparents take? All these influences affect society, they affect attitudes and parents' willingness or ability to care for their young. It is within that context that the authoritarian, democratic or permissive parent will be responsible for raising the generation that will eventually take care of ageing parents while nurturing its young.

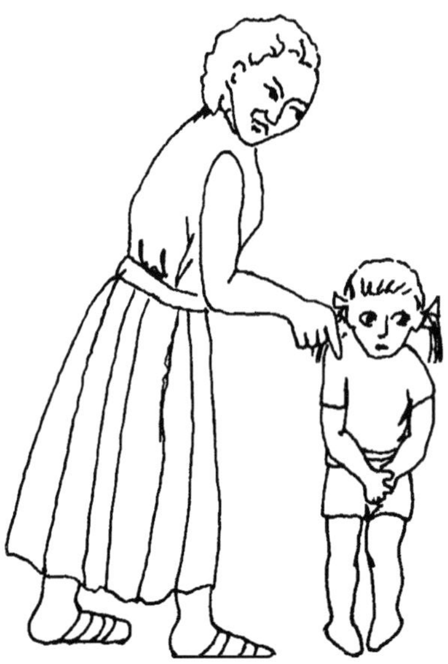

C. I'll be good if you give me an ice cream.	C. I'll be good if I can have an ice cream.	C. Do I have an ice cream or do I have a scene?
P. You'll never ever come out with me again. You are a very naughty boy/girl to even think such a thing	P. We are in a public place. If you can't behave here then we will leave.	P. What flavour would you like?
Dominating – put down	Firm – leave if necessary, it will only happen once or twice.	Conceding to bullying tactics. Child blackmails parents.
Labelling – rigid boundaries.	Most children try this at some time. It will only get worse if you let it.	No boundaries for child. How awful does this child have to become to be stopped?

Advice for Parents

Parenting Styles and Cultural Influence

1. Negotiate rules whenever possible.

2. Listen to your child's point of view.

3. Respect that point of view.

4. Give information about behaviour in informative ways when you are both calm.

5. Spend time playing with, or reading to, your child.

6. Allow them the chance to make choices in appropriate and safe ways.

7. Allow them age appropriate responsibilities.

8. Say "no" when you have to, explain why, stay with your decision.

9. Say "yes" if possible.

10. Be clear your self about who is making the decisions: you as an adult or the child you carry inside?

11. Be aware of the cultural climate your child operates in outside the family home.

Parents' Questions

Chapter 2 - Meeting Needs

1. Make a list of children's basic needs.

2. Are you able to meet all your children's needs?

3. Which of your basic needs were met when you were a child?

4. Were any not met?

5. How do you ensure your children's basic psychological needs are met?

6. Was there a time when, as a child, you felt unsafe?

7. Close your eyes and think of the safest place in your childhood home. Where was it? Why was it so safe?

8. Was there a time when you felt humiliated by a parent?

9. If the answer is yes, did it affect your relationship in any way?

Meeting Needs

Meeting your child's needs within the context of your own and the family's needs gives a very important message to your child. It says to your child "I respect the fact that you are an individual and have needs that are separate from mine". It also gives messages about valuing each family member. Children who have been given respect, felt valued and have in turn been able to give respect and understanding. They will be far better equipped to cope with the difficulties of the wider world than those who have experienced none of those opportunities.

In my experience one of the main reasons for things going wrong between parents and their children is that needs go unmet. This is no one's fault. The reasons why needs are not met can be many and complex. One way to avoid this happening is to put the relationship onto a needs met basis. It is never too late to do this and never too early to start. As a parent you are the person in control, you say to your child "what are your needs? These are my needs. How can we both feel satisfied?".

The Hierarchy of Human Needs

A humanistic psychologist, Abraham Maslow, developed a theory of a hierarchy of human need to explain not only the diversity of personal experience that is uniquely human, but also the motivational forces that drive our behaviour.

He looked at people who had been very successful in their lives, such as Thomas Jefferson, Einstein, Spinoza and Albert Schweitzer. He wanted to know what common factors these people shared. He discovered that they would be likely to have many of the following characteristics:

* they would be tolerant and accepting of others;
* they would have deeply satisfactory personal relationships;
* they themselves would be likely to be individualistic but not eccentric;
* they would be able to tolerate uncertainties;
* they would be able to take risks;
* they would take a problem-centred approach to life rather than a self-centred approach;
* they would have peak experiences.

The people most likely to be capable of peak experiences would be those who had the needs met that Maslow identified as essential if people were to become what he called self-actualising. The diagram on the next page encapsulates the natural progression of human needs very well.

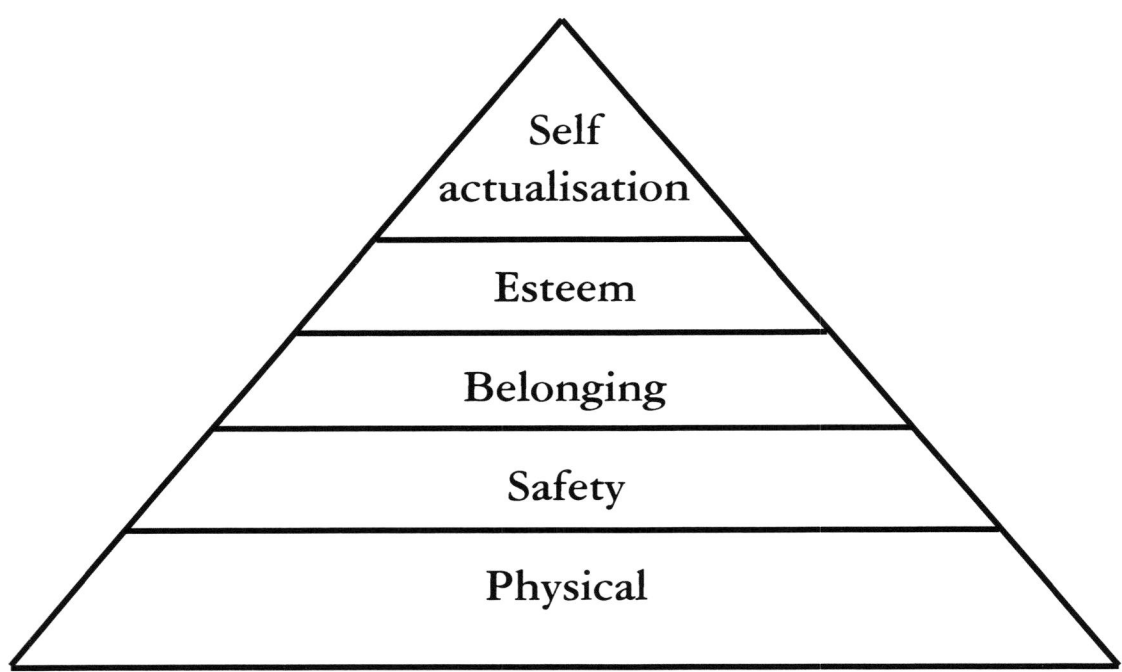

1. Physical

The first and most basic need a human has is for physical survival. Children need to be fed; they need shelter and warmth. The human being's need for food and drink continues throughout life. Feeding can become a battleground. I do not cover feeding as an isolated issue but it is mentioned within the context of behaviour management. Children need to have available to them enough food that is nourishing.

Other physical needs children have are for warm, appropriate clothing and shelter. Maslow sees these as absolutely fundamental and until they are met it is not possible to satisfactorily move on to the next stage.

What future then for the children in our society who are without their own homes? The many thousands who have been evicted or who have been born to parents living in bed and breakfast accommodation. How do those circumstances affect them? Certainly there have been enough reports to know that children in these circumstances suffer physically and educationally. We can only guess at the psychological damage because it does not always manifest in a way that draws the attention of people outside the home. It does however begin (or perpetuate) a cycle of very poor or unsatisfactory life experiences.

2. Safety

Children need to know that their homes and their food supply are safe. They need to be physically and emotionally safe. Children who are physically, emotionally or sexually abused are deprived of fundamental safety needs. Children living in unsatisfactory accommodation cannot feel very safe. Children living in the best homes in the country also may not feel especially safe if they are abused or neglected.

One mother, whose house provided plenty of material comforts, told me of how her daughter suddenly stopped wetting the bed when her eldest son left home. Apparently he had tried to smother her in a fit of temper one night, and for years her daughter had lived in fear that it would happen again. She had said nothing of it to her mother. The mother was horrified when she found out because she thought her children got along reasonably well. The child in this case had had her safety needs undermined by this incident.

3. Belonging

Children need to be part of a functioning social group. They need to have their places within that group. The first group they belong to is the family. If it is dysfunctional they may not have the experience of truly belonging. Some families create a 'family victim'. It is the child who is always naughty, always begins the arguments with siblings, and so on. Such a child will struggle to belong. When mother/child bonding has been poor the child may again struggle to belong.

Children who have not experienced belonging in a nuclear family will find it very difficult to fit in and belong in the wider society. Some families have a belief that within the context of local society they, in some way, do not fit in, or are outsiders. The children from these families are likely to have a self-image that reflects the family's view. All these children are in danger of becoming disaffected.

4. Esteem

Children need to have their talents and shortcomings accepted as part of their make-up. Self-esteem is developed through various channels as explained below. Our self-esteem will affect how we think of ourselves and how we believe we should behave. I discuss this important issue more fully in the chapter on self concept.

5. Self-actualisation

This is something every human is capable of. It is something that autonomous, independent personalities are most likely to achieve. Children need to be given a secure home base with the opportunities and the encouragement to practise life skills. If they make mistakes they need further encouragement, not condemnation.

All parents will say that they want their children to grow into responsible, caring and successful adults - even those who, at the same time, are using strategies that actually undermine their children's struggle to achieve those goals.

I intend saying very little about the baby years because there are many excellent baby books on the market; I would particularly recommend anything by Penelope Leach. As I have already indicated, this book is for the early to late childhood years and focuses mainly on the parent-child relationship.

Meeting the Needs from the Beginning

Unmet needs can happen at the very start of a baby's life. Each time I have been in hospital having my own children, I have been appalled at seeing teenage mothers being given contradictory advice on how to manage their babies. Each new nurse comes in with different attitudes, a different understanding of the situation and different ideas about how to remedy it. No wonder so few children are breast-fed. Instead of saying to young mums "take a few deep breaths and think about how you want to respond to your infant", they come in with feeding timetables, rules and restrictions that took them years to learn, expecting new mothers to instantly assimilate the information and put it into practice. Their advice is aimed at the "normal", "average" baby, wherever that might exist, with no allowances for the individuality and uniqueness of each mother and her baby. Each person has his or her own rhythm; each baby will grow into an adult who marches to the beat of their own drum. It is imperative to acknowledge that right at the start of life, and allow mothers and their new-born babies to settle into feeding rhythms that suit both of them.

The value of breast feeding a baby within minutes of its birth is now widely accepted. It not only provides the baby with the food and physical closeness it needs, but also with the psychological needs for the mother-child bonding. The early interference from "experts" (and, to an anxious, inexperienced mother, anyone who has had a baby or some training can appear to be an expert) can do untold damage. Problematic relationships can start at that time because a vulnerable mother, not confident enough in her own ability, can be dissuaded from following her intuition and in meeting the needs of her baby in her own unique way. Mothers need to be able to love and look after their babies. They need to feel they are nurturing them and enabling them to grow. Feeding their babies is a vital part of this process.

The only way babies can feel that security in love is through the way they are taken care of. They need to be held close, to be touched and cuddled. They need to feel secure and loved.

If the mother's ability to feed has been impaired or interrupted in some way, particularly by an "expert's" interference, the bonding between mother and infant may well be damaged.

When a baby cries it needs attention. You may or may not want to give that attention. Part of parenthood is attending to a baby's needs as soon as possible. If the child's needs can be met quickly it will save hours of frustration between you.
Parents hate to hear their infants cry. As the adults in control it is important to discover and assess the need. That involves an instinctive tuning in to the baby that both mothers and father's are capable of.

Most parents listen to the cries and are able to interpret what they mean; some will be able to distinguish between a cry that is for a wet nappy and the need for food, but not always. Also, each baby, even within the same family, is different. For example, one of my children never minded the feel of a wet or dirty nappy; it simply did not worry her. Another of my children hated even a spot of urine, let alone anything else, and needed an immediate change. One of my children went through a phase of crying on first waking. If I picked her up she would cry even more for quite some time. However, if I left her, the crying would subside after a few minutes, she would orientate herself, then be ready to be picked up.

Years ago mothers were told to feed wash and dress their infants then put them in prams at the bottom of the garden. This was done for hours at a time. It was considered necessary so that the mother could clean the house and prepare it for her husband's return home. The needs of the house and the father were put above the infant. Mothers were encouraged not to respond to their crying babies. It was thought that the child would be spoilt if it was cuddled often and given too much of mother's time. In recent years mothers have rebelled against that thinking and have taken an opposite view, submerging their own needs totally in their child's whims. Neither position is satisfactory. Unless we take a balanced approach and look at what everyone requires within the context of family life, we will continue to have dysfunctioning families with unhappy, dissatisfied and unfulfilled individuals unable to achieve their fullest potential.

When a small baby cries the reason is likely to be one of a few things such as:

* uncomfortable nappy or clothing
* hunger
* too hot/too cold
* wind
* illness
* need for company and/or a cuddle.

Babies do not cry just to annoy you. They have years to go before they acquire that concept. Their behaviour is very much at stimulus-response level. However, you can train your baby to cry unnecessarily, but that will usually be because its needs are not being met appropriately. You may not be able to find out exactly what is wrong and if your child is ill you may just have to bear with the noise. Usually if you attend to a crying baby quickly you can resolve the problem. You will set the expectation with your child that you will meet its needs, and later the payoff will be that your child will trust you enough to wait a few minutes if your track record is good.

There are exceptions to every single rule and some babies do cry endlessly for no apparent reason. The parents who lovingly care for such children are remarkable people. They have their relationship and patience stretched to their limits as they become increasingly tired and worn out. A colleague of mine worked with a mother who said that she never knew what giving was until she had a baby "because you have to give and give and give again even when you don't want to". The task of caring for an endlessly crying infant will seem never-ending and without thanks. The patient loving is repaid later, because a child who experiences love will have love to give later.

Meeting Needs as Children Grow

Babies' needs are relatively straightforward and uncomplicated. As children grow older the situation becomes less clear. It is important to be clear about the difference between **needs** and **wants**. A reminder from Maslow will be useful. Below are the first four:

Physical	shelter that is warm and dry, appropriate clothing and food
Safety	to live in homes that offer physical and emotional safety
Belonging	to belong inside the family home and to belong in the society outside the home
Esteem	to be loved and valued as a unique individual

These are the basic needs for any child, more than that is a bonus. Children from very poor environments can grow up feeling very strong as individuals, emotionally ready to cope with life, capable of being altruistic, co-operative and socially responsive to the world. Whereas it is possible to have children from very privileged backgrounds growing up with very little emotional strength, unable to co-operate, remaining egocentric and not being very socially responsive. The behaviour of some young people from such backgrounds makes the tabloid headlines from time to time. There is also interesting research evidence where children from such backgrounds have been compared with one another. For example the work of Nancy and Theodore Graves (1974, 1983), provides insight into the influence of child rearing practices and social contexts in which children live. Money and material things are not what children need. As we have seen their needs are for safety, security and physical and emotional nurturing.

Many parents worry desperately about providing the latest toy or particular brand of clothes. It is unnecessary. Their children asking may drive the worries, but they are wants as opposed to needs. One mother I know refused to pay the £90 required for some brand name trainers. Instead she gave her son a small allowance; she contributed £30 to his new trainers and made him pay the difference if he wanted anything more expensive. She did this with other clothes as well. His desire for expensive brand name goods has gone and he is accruing a healthy bank balance. Children do not need such things to survive physically or emotionally, they do need parental time, attention and love. As they grow they also need to be part of an accepting friendship group. They need to be in a school that meets their academic needs and fosters a positive, realistic image of their abilities and themselves as people. I hear many parents bemoan the materialistic, selfish society we live in yet they perpetuate those same values by encouraging a huge number of needs that are really only wants. Referring back to Maslow's list will be helpful.

Advice for Parents

Meeting Needs

1. A baby has needs that can only be conveyed through crying. Attend to a crying baby as soon as possible.

2. A baby needs to see and feel the closeness of a parent. Holding, touching and talking are vital.

3. Sucking is also an early need.

4. Needs met at an early age will encourage a more patient and trusting child later on.

5. Attention through, for example, showing interest and giving time, is of more value than anything bought in the shops.

6. Where possible discuss your child's perceived needs and set them within the context of the family. This shows that everyone is valued.

Parents' Question Page

Chapter 3 - Self Concept

Ask yourself:

1. Would you say you were a confident person?

2. Are you more confident in different situations?

3. Think back to your own childhood. Who made you feel good about yourself?

4. How did they do that?

5. Think of your parents' faces. How do you remember them looking at you when you were a child? Are they usually smiling at you with approval?

6. Do you remember yourself as a good child or a naughty child?

7. Who gave you that view of yourself?

8. How do you feel about giving good positive messages to your child?

9. How do you encourage your child to have a positive self-image and protect their self-image?

Self Concept

The words self-image, self-esteem, self-concept are in common usage these days, but what exactly do they mean? They basically mean the view we have of ourselves, our worth and the beliefs we hold about our potential. The way this view is built and developed is complex, it is very important because it has a large part to play in determining how we behave. Self-concept is, according to Denis Lawrence (1987), an umbrella term. Within it sits what is known as self-image and ideal-self, the two together equal self-esteem. It can be illustrated in this way.

Self-concept is:

$$\text{Self-image} + \text{Ideal-self} = \text{Self-esteem}$$

Self Image

When your baby is born, the way you react to it, how often you smile and cuddle it, how you help it cope with the world and the way you set limits for it, will all help your child develop a self-image. Other people also contribute to that self-image, such as the frequent visitors to your home, your friends and relatives. Later, your child's friends and teachers will all have an impact, as will the child's inborn personality. Your child will be given information about herself, such as how fat/thin, good/naughty, loveable/unloveable, and so on, she is. As she grows she will compare that information with similar information given to brothers and sisters or other children such as cousins and friends. She will also know from sources such as television, what is good and not so good information to receive about herself within the context of society at large. With all that information she will form an opinion about herself, she will make a decision on what sort of person she is. The basis for that opinion begins at home, in the family. The earliest and most important source of information about self-image is you.

If your child lives with constant criticism, is constantly given negative messages for example about abilities or looks then it will grow up with a very poor self-image. If you tell your child regularly enough that it is naughty, it is clumsy, it is horrid, it is messy, it is unable to do this or that, it will believe you. After all, do you tell lies? Of course not. Your child will believe that it is as you say it is. Once it is developed and shaped, self-image is very stubborn and difficult to alter, it likes to hang on to what it knows even if it is all bad and negative. The words you use, the way you react to your child will have a very powerful influence on the positive or negative self-image your child carries with it.

Ideal Self

This is the child's goals and aspirations. It is developing at the same time as the self-image and they interact with one another. The child or any person who is significant in a child's life can set the goals. Parents are usually the earliest influence, however, as soon as the child comes into contact with others such as friends at nursery, teachers and so on, then they start to compare themselves and their lives. They begin to have aspirations. If the goals are realistic and, with some effort, attainable, all will be well. If they are unrealistic and unattainable then problems may arise and the child may give up. Having goals set at an optimum level is important because goals that are too easy and present no challenge are not worthy targets. They lead to laziness or complacency.

An example of unrealistic goals being set, that did not match self-image, was what happened to Jonathan. He was a brilliant artist. He could do characters of children in his class and his teachers with amusing accuracy. This ability held no interest for his parents. His father was an accountant and had his own business, which he hoped his son would go into. Jonathan was of average ability at maths but he certainly had no intention of following his father. His parents' lack of support and inability to value their son's talent and disregard of his wishes led to him feeling a failure at life in general. His father was only interested in Jonathan's grades in maths - these deteriorated. He lost interest in drawing. He did almost no work yet managed to get an A in his exams, but he said what was the use of an A in art? Because his parents were refusing to allow him to follow a career that interested him and used his natural talent, he was unable to motivate himself to do anything and relations at home became very strained.

After some outside help in the form of family counselling, the issues were understood. Jonathan's father believed a career in art to be frivolous and very unstable. However he eventually supported his son and allowed him to attend Art College. Jonathan went on to become a very wealthy advertising executive in the eighties, providing his father's firm with a very important business account.

Self Esteem

This is the conclusion a child - or indeed an adult - comes to when the information about self-image is balanced with that of the ideal-self. There needs to be some challenge set at the right level between self-image and ideal-self. There must be goals that require some work, but they must be attainable. The child must have a sufficiently positive self-image to believe the goals can be attained.

The combination of a positive self-image with realistic goals for making a positive ideal-self will result in high self-esteem and overall a strong self-concept. Children with high self-concept will feel good about themselves and feel confident to take risks such as to tackle tasks they are unfamiliar with. This is very important not only for scholastic success, but success in life generally. Children with a positive, confident self-concept are more likely to do well at school. One reason for this is that if they get things wrong they are more likely to believe that they can put things right, and will have the confidence to ask for help from teachers. If they have a low self-concept they are more likely to feel that they can never get things right. They will believe that this is how life is for them, they are poor performers and that there is nothing they can do to improve. They are also unlikely to ask for help because they will lack the confidence to do so.

Parents' Contribution

Remember the two components of self-esteem: the self-image and the ideal-self. The main contribution that you, the parent, makes to these components, is the words you use to your child and the way you react with the demands, limitations and sanctions you impose. While early parenting is a significant factor in developing self-concept, it is important to say it is not the only determining factor over the adult self-concept. It is possible for children to survive apparently extremely detrimental circumstances and recover, to become secure in their self-worth, fully self-actualizing in the way I described earlier. Nathan Branden (1992:58) says these children are likely to have "strategic detachment". By this he means

> *"They somehow know, this is not all there is. They hold the belief that a better alternative exists somewhere and that some day they will find their way to it. They persevere in that idea. They somehow know Mother is not all women, Father is not all men, this family does not exhaust the possibilities of human relationships - there is life beyond this neighbourhood. This does not spare them suffering in the present, but it allows them not to be destroyed by it. Their strategic detachment does not guarantee that they will never know feelings of powerlessness, but it helps them not to be stuck there."*

Children with strategic detachment are likely to become the adults who survive a childhood that damages, rather than nurtures, a healthy self-concept. Children from all walks of life enter adulthood with unhelpful, unhealthy, negative images of themselves. Some continue through life with these views, others move on. Parents themselves may have left childhood with unhelpful views of their worth and abilities. It may be a part of the cycle of inherited family patterning. The blueprint that is passed from generation to generation. "I became very aware of this blueprint when I heard my parents and grandparent talking to my children; it stirred memories in me.

Recent years have seen a greater understanding of self-concept, Branden (1992:12) says that: *"people possessing a decent level of self-esteem are now needed economically in large numbers. Historically this is a new phenomenon."* Maybe this is why more is known about self-concept. Whatever the reason, parents have acquired the responsibility of guardians and nurturers of their child's self-concept while their children are dependent on them. Mental health is as important as physical health.

Labelling

A common mistake is name-calling or labelling a child. Calling children names in order to make them stop a particular behaviour is a common tactic of permissive or authoritarian parents. Many children take these names to heart and consider themselves labelled. This makes matters much, much worse. If you have called your child a bully, a baby, a wimp, naughty, a show-off, or any one of a thousand possibilities, it is likely that your child will believe the label and will repeat the performance that got them the label in the first place.

The words we use and the responses we make to our children's behaviour are very powerful tools. They help children understand how the world sees them, and helps them to understand the sort of personality they are developing. If you are constantly trying to alter your child's behaviour by name calling, you are likely to be actually reinforcing that behaviour. Phrases such as:
* "He's always silly and shows off when we have visitors"
* "You're such a baby"
* "You're clumsy when you wash up"

will have the effect of reinforcing and encouraging the behaviour. I can almost guarantee that you will have a child showing off each time you have visitors if you reinforce their behaviour in that way, and how can you possibly continue to ask a clumsy child to wash up?

Good Girls, Bad Boys

Society is very often responsible for creating good girls and bad boys. I have lost count of how many times I have been told that so-and-so is "a typical boy". I usually ask parents what that means. The reply is fairly standard, with words like naughty, a pest, boisterous, and into everything. When I watch and listen to the way these people manage their boy children, it very often becomes clear that they are encouraging anti-social, naughty or aggressive behaviour.

> *Recently I was visiting a young woman and when I first arrived she was not at home. Her mother let me into the house saying her daughter would be along presently but she was collecting her son from playgroup. As we chatted she proudly told me that her grandson was a "typical boy, into everything", and her granddaughter was "a lovely, quiet, obedient child".*
> *Eventually the young woman arrived home. She came in with her two children. The little girl went and sat at a table to occupy herself while we were talking. Her grandmother commented on how good she was and she was doing just what she should expect of her. The grandmother then turned her attention to her grandson. "Here's grandma's little pest" she said, giving him a cuddle. "Into everything he is, takes not a blind bit of notice. You'll see, he'll have that pot out all over the place in a minute". With that she put him down and right on cue he tipped over a small pot on the table in front of us. She told him not to, called him her little pest again and reminded me about the accuracy of her prediction. She then went on to list more likely "misdemeanours" and he duly performed. Meanwhile the granddaughter sat quietly fulfilling the role set for her.*

All the words of condemnation were said with warmth, sometimes with a hug, and sometimes a smile. This little boy was slowly and carefully being moulded into a "typical" boy, i.e. a wilful, rude, aggressive child. His sister was also being moulded into a "typical" girl - quiet, obedient and passive.

The "moulding" was being done with words, looks, tone of voice and body language. It has long been recognised that this is how we encourage children. What people seem unconscious of is how deliberately and consistently they create the gender differences. At playgroup I used to become quite agitated to hear mothers saying to their infants that they could not do a particular activity because they were a boy or a girl. It is in the home that violent criminals are made in most cases. It is during childhood that the seeds of problematic adult relationships are sown. It is in very early childhood that we begin to understand who we are, and what sort of personality we possess, even before we are able to articulate it; and it is words and actions such as those described above that enable a child to develop an image of themselves. If the way we behave and react to children is faulty, then so will be their understanding of themselves and the world around them.

Treat your child's self-concept as you do their physical health. Self-concept is a key element in their mental health. You ensure your child receives enough food and exercise to ensure a healthy body; self-concept needs the equivalent. The exercise comes from good, well set goals that are achieved by some effort. The food is in the information you 'feed' into them. Trust that your children will achieve. Reward and praise effort. Celebrate success, differences, their love and their uniqueness. Express confidence in them, tell them they are loveable, likeable, fun and that you are pleased to have them as your children.

The Jesuit priests used to say "Give me the child until he is seven, and I will give you the man". Being a parent is a powerful position to be in. You have your children from birth. You have the power to contribute to the next generation, for better or worse, because your child's self-concept will drive their behaviour. A loved, well-nurtured, disciplined self-concept will give a loving well-balanced, self-disciplined individual.

Below is an acronym P.R.E.P. to help remind you of what is needed to help young children on the road to a confident self-image. Patience is needed when anything new is being learnt and life skills are no exception. Reassurance and encouragement help the learning to be less traumatic, and praise for a successful outcome will increase the chance of success again.

> **P** ⇒ **Patience**
> **R** ⇒ **Reassurance**
> **E** ⇒ **Encouragement**
> **P** ⇒ **Praise**

Reinforcing the Self-Concept

It is possible for a child to be in a self-reinforcing upward or downward spiral of good or poor self-concept because:

What is said to a child about itself affects

The way a child thinks; which affects

self-concept

The way she feels; which affects

The way she behaves; which affects

The way that others feel about the child; which affects

The way that they behave towards the child; which affects

Advice for Parents

Developing Self-Esteem

1. Whenever possible, look kindly and lovingly at your child, give a smile as often as possible.

2. Never call them names.

3. Listen to them when they have problems.

4. Be supportive and encouraging.

5. Show genuine interest.

6. Acknowledge difficulties they have.

7. Label their behaviour as unacceptable - never them.

Parents' Questions

Chapter 4 - Sibling Rivalry

Ask yourself:

1. Do your children argue?

2. If yes, do you feel they argue more than most other brothers and sisters?

3. Did you have a sister or brother with whom to argue as a child?

4. Were there times when it was worse than others, such as moments of real hate and anger?

5. Did your parents intervene?

6. If yes, did their interventions ever make matters better or worse?

7. If your answer to Question 5 is no, do you wish they had intervened?

8. Have you ever discussed this aspect of your childhood with your now adult siblings?

9. If yes, were their memories and perceptions of what went on the same as yours?

10. If your answer to Question 8 is no, could you discuss childhood rivalries with your siblings, or are they still there in adulthood?

11. If your answer to Question 1 is yes, do your interventions improve matters in the long term? If so, how?

12. If your answer to Question 1 is yes, do your interventions make matters worse?

13. When your children fight, how do you feel?

Sibling Rivalry

Almost every family with more than one child experiences sibling rivalry. A perennial problem for parents, it usually surfaces at most inconvenient times. There is a wonderful book entitled Siblings without Rivalry, by A Faber and E Mazlish(1988), that deals expertly with this issue, and I recommend it to all parents. Within the confines of this chapter I will attempt to highlight some of the causes of rivalry and some useful ways to deal with it.

If you had brothers or sisters there is a 99% chance that you experienced sibling rivalry. The pain, jealousy, anger, fear or other emotion can, in my experience, go to the grave with some people. It can prevent not only satisfactory adult sibling relationships, but satisfactory relationships of any sort. Sibling rivalry can be a very destructive force throughout a person's entire life. Maybe the questions at the beginning of this struck a chord with you? One of the greatest problems for siblings and the rivalry they experience is their parents! Parental interference in the actual incidents can, and often does, exacerbate the problem. Also the way the children are dealt with generally, such as comparisons made, the encouragement of competition, teasing, name calling, and taking sides, can all lead to hurt feelings that deepen the rivalry between brothers and sisters.

> *Often the problems start at the very beginning. When I was pregnant with my second baby I was having coffee with a friend when an elderly neighbour came in. She cooed at my eldest child, who was just over three years old at the time, "I bet you are excited at having a brother or sister to play with soon". When she had gone my friend observed "Why do we talk such garbage to children? It'll be years before they are able to play together, saying things like that sets up expectations that cannot happen and then disappoints the child". How right she was. I was not at all surprised when a few days after Chloe's brother was born she said with some exasperation "Well how long will I have to wait to play with him then?"*

At that age children are very much in touch with their feelings. They give parents the right clues to pick up. Unfortunately parents often rush in with roadblocks (see the chapter on listening). Examples are:

Child   *"I hate her."*

Mother   *"Oh, you don't feel that way about your sister."*

Denial of child's feelings by interpreting:

> *"You're a silly thing to say things you know you don't feel."* (name calling and incorrect interpretation)

> *"You mustn't think like that, it's naughty, you'll upset your mummy."* (moralising)

Reassuring and diverting are two more common roadblocks used with young children. Reassurance is often used to make the adult feel better, for example if parents argue and the child asks "What's the matter?" and the reply is "Nothing", that stops any further communication but it can be confusing and worrying for a child when patently there is something the matter. Diverting is a very useful trick for small children when we need to divert them to another area of interest, but not when it blocks much needed communication. Moving on to another topic of conversation, or remembering something they should have done, will divert but what ever the difficulty is it will have to be confronted at sometime.

Imagine the elder child, often little more than a baby, coping with feelings of intense jealousy. Not only is there probably no one to share those feelings with, but also there is no way of understanding what those feelings really are or why they are there. The child is then told that those feelings are naughty or that they do not exist, or that in reality they feel something else. Confusing? I should say so! Is it any wonder that those feelings go underground to surface later when the replacement baby becomes mobile, starts wearing the elder child's clothes and playing with their toys? Seen in that light, the new interloper's behaviour becomes more outrageous as time goes on.

When young, my children had times when they would put their arms around me and declare, "My mummy, no one else's, all mine," or they would say, "Let's pretend that it's just you and me, no other children". My response to that was always "I am mummy to all of you, you can pretend in your own head, but I can't play that game". I believe it is threatening to play that sort of game with children because it could be their turn to be excluded next. It is important to allow for differences and uniqueness in your children and to steadfastly love them for it. It is also helpful in the prevention of rivalry if you can encourage your children to value themselves and each other's separate identities. It is OK to say to your children, "I love each of you differently because you are different, unique people. You are all equally valuable to me, but, because you are each your own person, I have to love you each separately and respond as you need me to."

I have three children, they are all very different. My husband and I celebrate their differences with words like "Its really lovely to have children who are so different, you all bring different interests into the house, and because of you we are learning about so many things. We think its really exciting." We emphasise the value of their uniqueness and the fact that we want them to explore their own paths through life in their own ways. We are there to support and encourage them.

Fighting

Fights can become a way of attracting your attention. Bogus fighting can be used by one child to draw your anger onto another. For example, if you wade in to stop the 'fight' and are in the habit of blaming one child over another, then you may find that the 'good' child is setting the 'bad' child up. You will be used like a pawn if you are not careful. This was a trap I fell into myself, and I have witnessed it in many families. If your intervention on one side is virtually guaranteed then it would be a mature child indeed who did not use it to their advantage when things were not going their way. How can brothers and sisters love each other under these circumstances?

When intervention is necessary in your child's problem use reflective responses explained in the section on listening skills. Remember who owns the problem - not you - the bad feelings are your children's. Do not rush in with solutions, they may work only for you. Trust your children to deal with the problem and to find a resolution. If they are hurting one another it is then that you may need to intervene, split them up, put them in separate rooms and then encourage them to talk once each has calmed down.

Equal Treatment?

"Children don't need to be treated equally. They need to be treated uniquely," say Faber and Mazlish. One mother I know even resorted to writing down in a book exactly what she had given her two children to prove to them that they were being treated equally and being given the same amount of things. You cannot treat your children equally, their perceptions and experience of life cannot be the same.

The early life experience of a first-born child will be entirely different to that of second and subsequent children. The dynamics between you and your partner will change with a first baby, then when the next baby arrives the family dynamics will alter again. One big difference between child one and child two will be time allocation to the new baby. The mother will be spreading her time between two demanding children. She may also be working. Both parents will be lacking in sleep. The first child may perceive themselves as slipping down the pecking order for attention. With each new addition to the family, the dynamics change, thus altering the life experiences of those within the family. To parents who say to their children in later years "You all had the same experience" or "You were all treated the same" I say, wait a minute, think back: did they really have the same experience? No! Life is a constantly evolving and changing process. It is important to understand the different quality of experience each child will have in your family. You will not be in a position to treat them all the same. The life experience each child will have may be different, but that does not mean to say it will be better or worse, just unique - as indeed each child is.

Competition

There is a belief among some people in our society that competition is good for children, that it is character building. The latter may have some limited mileage. Children do not need adult, structured competition. They are competitive enough on their own. Competition is the antithesis to co-operation and sharing - competition means winners and losers. It works while you are on the winning team. If you want a loving family where sharing and co-operation are predominant features then eschew competition within the family at all costs. Competition between siblings will arise naturally, and it can be difficult to handle. Encouraged by parents it can be poisonous and destructive. It can lead to damaged personalities, relationships and destroyed lives. Competition between family members has no place in the maturation of loving relationships. The family should be the place where children learn to value themselves, to value other family members, and to appreciate and celebrate differences. That will be difficult, if not impossible, in a family where individual members are in competition with one another.

Deal one to one

Deal one to one, never compare one child with another. Always focus on the issue with the individual concerned. It is acceptable to compare a child's own past achievements with what is currently happening, but not with anyone else. If one child's bedroom is in a mess and you want it cleared, deal one to one. Do not compare it with others. For example, an excellent way to fuel sibling rivalry would be to say something like this:
"Your brother's room is always so tidy, why can't you keep it like him?"
when what would be more helpful would be:
" I know you can make your room look so tidy, would you like some help or would you prefer to do it on your own?"
Of course this is not offering a choice about whether the job is to be done or not, but you are offering help in a situation that may feel out of control to your child. Sometimes they allow the mess to build up until the job of sorting it out becomes just too much. You are also comparing a past achievement with one that is about to happen. Do not compare one child's school report with another. Each child's school experience will be unique. You may find they even have different responses to different teachers. Each child should be compared only with his or her own past record.

Summary

Even in the calmest of households children will spend some time arguing. How much time and how ferocious those arguments become and whether they are resolved or continue into adulthood, will depend on how they are managed. To a very large extent they will depend on you. Children's battles will trigger emotions in you. Be aware of what happens to your emotions. When your children fight how do you feel? What are your motives when you intervene, or not? Is your intervention driven by the adult parent or the child within you?

> *One father I know fought constantly (not physically but emotionally) with his sister when they were young. He was forbidden to touch her, she was allowed to hit him. When he had his own two children he constantly told his daughter that she was like her aunt, while he saw himself in his son. He usually intervened on his son's behalf, name calling his daughter. It was not unknown for him to call her "a little bitch", "spiteful" and so on. It was only when he gained some insight into his behaviour that he was able to become more objective when his two children fought. He was able to deal with them in an adult way, mediating and problem solving rather than rushing in with hurtful name calling.*

How valuable is your intervention?

Advice for Parents
Sibling Rivalry

Preventive work:

1. Celebrate when things are going well between them.
2. Show by example and teach respect for others' uniqueness.
3. Value each other's differences, by celebrating the fact that your children are different. Enjoy it.
4. Encourage self-worth and self-respect.
5. You do not own all your children's interactions with each other.
6. Encourage co-operation and sharing, never competition.
7. Remember, you do not own your children's feelings, they belong to them.
8. Be honest, don't play games.

When problems occur:

1. Listen to both sides - use reflective responses - acknowledge the hurt on both sides.
2. Whenever possible trust them to sort out the problem - tell them you trust them.
3. Ask for their advice on how you should resolve the problems.
4. Give them time (especially if you are trying to change a pattern that has built up over several years - you will not change it overnight).
5. Explain that you can order them to stop causing each other pain but they really have to resolve it for themselves to live happily together, because you can't be in the room with them all the time.

Parents' Questions

Chapter 5 - Difficulties for Parents

1. List the difficulties you can see a parent might encounter for themselves.

2. What difficulties might children give you?

3. What other problems are there for parents to encounter?

4. Who could help you through those difficulties? List all the people you know you can call on.

5. How can you prepare yourself for the problems of parenthood?

6. Read the chapter. How did your list match to mine?

Difficulties for Parents

The range of potential difficulties is as varied and numerous as humanity itself. This chapter will briefly discuss two broad areas. They are:

a) difficulties that I believe are "within parents", the emotional baggage that parents bring to the role of parenting;

b) the difficulties that are "within children", such as those children who are born with exceptional problems, such as mental or physical handicap.

Difficulties within Parents

Throughout the book parents are encouraged to address old patterns of behaviour and beliefs that they carry with them as an internal mental picture of what a parent is, and how a parent should react in any given situation. The questions used at the beginning of some chapters have been designed to help adults think about their expectations as parents, what their internal role models are, where they came from and whether they are still useful and so on.

Over the years that I have spent working with parents whose children have been perceived as having behavioural or emotional problems, I have come to understand just how many people are what I call "reactive parents". That is, they have not thought about this role of parenting, or considered the issues. From day to day, month to month, year in, year out, they simply react to situations without ever questioning their own behaviour or the internal role model that they use. They constantly repeat long established family patterns that should have been discarded generations ago. Poor family patterns may include:

* marital discord
* early bonding problems
* too harsh punishments
* emotional and physical neglect
* unresolved extended family discord

There can be other stresses on family life such as chronic illness, a physically or mentally handicapped family member. Poor or overcrowded housing in areas where crime is high may also lead to poor parenting, as can problems such as drug and alcohol misuse. Unemployment can also damage family relationships.

Poor quality relationships between parents can lead to children developing equally poor relationships based on the role models they have observed and experienced.

The appearance of a new baby is more likely to exacerbate any problems than resolve them. Children are very hard work - the physical demands of looking after them, loss of sleep in the early days, and so on. If parents are already struggling with their relationship the extra work having a child involves will not help.

Parents who are needful individuals for example, whose early needs went unmet, are unlikely to be able to respond adequately to a demanding, helpless infant, the robust wilful toddler, and the growing child.

Loss: Divorce and Death

Loss and/or separation can also cause problems for children. Divorce and death are the two main problems. In recent years I have seen several children suffering from unresolved loss of grandparents. There has been even more suffering from parents' marital break-up. I have come to believe that, for children, divorce can sometimes be more difficult to come to terms with than death. Children of divorced parents always seem to hold the belief that "while there's life there's hope". They cling to the hope that their parents will get together again. It is rare for a child to come to terms with the split. Children are forgotten. Parents go to marriage guidance counselling and get other help - children just become naughty. I am not saying that once partners have children they should never separate, that would be unrealistic. What I am saying is that the pain and sense of loss that children feel with each new turn of events should be recognised and understood. Parents, fathers in particular in my experience, undervalue how very important they are to their children. However acrimonious or painful the split, the two partners remain the biological parents of their children. That can never change. Those two people - MUM and DAD- have a special place in their children's hearts that no one else can ever have in quite the same way. It needs to be acknowledged and allowed for. The pain for all involved needs to be recognised and openly discussed, and this will allow the anger and grief to be exposed and explored. It will not be easy or comfortable but it will speed recovery. Unresolved anger and grief is unhealthy. It reappears in other ways. An example of how this happens can be seen in Angela's story. She had unresolved issues concerning death and divorce to contend with.

> *I was asked by a school to see a young girl of ten, who had, over a period of 18 months, become increasingly difficult and violent. I visited her mum who told me about her divorce. She was also finding Angela difficult, she felt she was losing her. She blamed herself. The first time I saw Angela she told me within a few minutes that her Gran had died. She was unclear about when this had happened, but it was recently. She drew me a picture of her family that included Gran. On my next visit to see her mother I asked about Gran. Her mother was astonished. The Gran had died almost 3 years earlier. Until her sudden death she had seen Angela daily. Angela was not allowed to go to the funeral. She was taken to the grave once and because she was upset and cried, she was not taken again. Gran was not talked about for fear of upsetting her. Angela's mother felt that she had not grieved for her mother because within weeks of her death her*

own marriage ran into difficulties resulting in divorce. She had lived alone with her daughter for about a year.

I explained that Angela was stuck in grief and that part of the healing process probably involved some tears. Angela was allowed a photograph of her Gran, she and her mother visited the grave and they cried together as they talked about their memories of her.

Our next area to work on together was the divorce of her parents. I visited Angela's father. He had never talked about the divorce to anyone. I encouraged him to talk to his daughter. She had heard her mother's version, she wanted to hear her father's. To her surprise they both told the same story: they no longer loved one another but they loved her. One of Angela's abiding fears was that if her parents could fall out of love with one another then they could just as easily stop loving her. Now that her Gran was gone who was there to turn to? Angela continued to test the endurance of their love for some while. Her behaviour settled in school. When I last saw her she was 14 years old. She had accepted the divorce, was pleased that her mum had a partner and was doing well in school.

Many children fear that their parents' love may be fickle enough to exclude them in the future, they often secretly believe that they were responsible for the divorce. Sometimes it is very difficult to shake this belief in their guilt.

I worked for over a year with Malcom before he confided in me that it was his direct intervention that forced his father to leave. His memory was that during one of his parents' arguments he came between them and said he was fed up with all the rows. His father then said he would leave, and never returned. When I told this to his parents they had no recollection of the incident. We all met in my office together, and for the first time they explained to Malcom why they had split. He needed to have reminders from time to time. His truancy stopped and his grades in school gradually improved.

Early Bonding Problems

Bonding simply means the love and attachment between parents and their children. It is something many parents begin while the baby is in the womb, for others it happens once the baby is born as they love and look after a helpless infant. In recent years fathers have been encouraged to become involved as early as possible with the nurturing of their babies because it helps with the emotional attachment.

Bonding may not happen in a satisfactory way for a variety of reasons. For example, one or both parents may not have experienced a satisfactory emotional attachment themselves. This can be particularly devastating for a child if it is the mother who was not nurtured as a child and therefore cannot know how to nurture in return. It is possible for fathers to compensate. If the parents' relationship is in difficulty, or if there is illness in the family, there may not be enough time or emotional energy to bond. If the financial situation does not allow the mother to take enough time away from work there may be difficulties.

The possible reasons why bonding can be prevented or interrupted are too many to list. The early bonding is crucial to mother and child, although fathers can fill the nurturing mother role just as well. It lays the foundations for the future. A house built without good foundations will crack, have crooked bits, and be unsafe. So it is for children. The early bonding forms part of the foundations. It is essential that the nurturing relationship between a mother and her baby be protected. This is a father's first nurturing role.

A family that has given the baby the experience of good bonding is unlikely then to neglect, or abuse emotionally, physically or sexually. Sadly, it does occasionally happen. Once again it is more likely to occur if parents experienced any neglect or abuse. It can also occur for all the reasons listed previously. Families that find themselves isolated, without friends or family, can be very vulnerable. Unsupported young girls or emotionally immature adults may not have the strength to cope with the demands that a young child makes. If early bonding has been a problem then the child's behaviour is likely to be a cause for concern. Advice found in the chapter on Serious Misbehaviours will be useful.

Difficulties Within Children

Some children are very difficult to bond with. This can be for a variety of reasons, usually having a physical or mental basis. Some very premature babies are kept in incubators for weeks and months, with parents unable to hold and cuddle and do all the things one normally does with a baby. Children who are very slow to feed, who suffer from colic, who do not sleep, who cry for no apparent reason, can be very hard to love and nurture. Children who need a great deal of medical attention can also be difficult for some parents to bond with, because they feel that the professionals take over.

This book is not about particular handicaps. There are a number of identified conditions or syndromes that can cause strains on the family. In Appendix 1, I discuss two difficulties that cause enormous emotional and social problems for parents. Parents of children with these problems often describe them as causing relationship strains for the whole family.

Dealing With Professionals - Another Difficulty

As a parent one's practise at this starts right at the beginning. As soon as a woman's doctor knows she is pregnant, the state health machine swings into action. For the sake of the physical health of women and babies this is no bad thing at all. However, the whole process can be extremely difficult to cope with on an emotional level, largely due to the "omnipotent professional" or doctor/gods. Hanna Corbishley, as national secretary to the National Childbirth Trust, put it very well:

> *"As a parent I was often in the position of submissiveness to the omnipotent professional - the doctor or headmaster who seems to balance your child's life and future in his hands. You can argue about issues concerning yourself but it is hard to argue about your child.*

However well reasoned or carefully researched your arguments, rational thought flies out of the window when such strong emotions take over, and professionals must remember how vulnerable parents are when an issue concerning their child is at stake."

Hanna Corbishley is clearly an articulate professional, but when the issue is close to home, i.e. one's self, partner or child, the emotional intensity is such that it may be difficult to be rational and objective. Even when one can remain cool and in control it is my experience that some professionals retrench even further behind jargon and their "expertise" in the face of probing, information-seeking questions. They are threatened when they meet people who are their intellectual and academic peers, and can pick their way through the jargon and question the basis of decisions that are made. It means that they have to justify themselves and that they cannot have their own way because of incomprehension or blind faith. Also, if parents insist on understanding issues then some of the professionals' power (usually called expertise or mystique) evaporates as it is shared with others.

As a professional, I found the business of having a baby, and the aftercare, salutary in terms of understanding how I should behave when talking with parents. I hope it improved my manners and presentation, and that I no longer put other parents in the same position that I felt myself to be in, and that Hanna Corbishley describes.
Many professionals and experts have not had the opportunity to gain such insights, and continue to disempower parents.

If your child has a problem of any sort, find out as much as you can, read, contact action groups, talk to other parents, make yourself as knowledgeable as possible. Then you will be informed enough to ask questions and discuss issues with the experts you are seeing. You will also be able to make joint decisions, based on your expert knowledge of your child and your family and professional experts about how you want the situation managed.

Summary

Being a parent is, as I have already said, unremittingly hard work. It is not as straightforward as the advertising world would have us believe. In this book I try to help parents refuse to repeat unhelpful patterns of past generations. I also try to steer them through a loving course with their children. Parents bring with them all the hurts they suffered as children, they have all the good times as well. Try to get in touch with that child within you and remember the fear, shame, humiliations and hurts. It won't be a comfortable experience, but it may help you to stop it from happening to your own child, for whom you have such high hopes.

If you are the parent of a physically or mentally handicapped child, to a large extent the same rules apply for achieving the sort of home environment needed that I discuss throughout this book.

Advice for Parents

Difficulties For Parents

1. Consistency from both parents, where possible, on agreed rules and routines will help.

2. Parents offering a positive role model in terms of how they respond to their children and each other.

3. Parents who are able to give love and unconditional acceptance to their children and each other.

4. Security with parents who are comfortable with each other and, if at all possible, free of excessive stress and tensions (see Maslow's hierarchy, Chapter 2).

5. Provision of the basic needs (see Maslow's hierarchy, Chapter 2).

6. As much openness and honesty as possible.

7. Seek advice when you need it.

8. Do not be afraid to ask questions of professionals. It is part of their job to explain matters in a way that you can understand.

Meeting the basic needs for food, warmth, shelter and love, along with the safety and security of a loving home will help children to grow into happy secure individuals who are ready to bring up another generation with good parenting skills.

Parents' Questions

Chapter 6 - Rules And Values

1. Are you aware of consciously:
   (a) rejecting any of your parents' values?
   (b) Adopting any of your parent's values?

2. Can you think about how your parents' rules reflected their values?

3. Write down the rules you believe you follow in your home:
   a) for mealtimes
   b) for keeping the house tidy
   c) for cooking, washing up, etc.

4. We have rules, unwritten, often unspoken, in all areas of our lives. List some of your parents' rules that irritated you.

5. List rules of your mother's/father's that you consciously changed, and those you kept, when you had your own home.

6. Ask your partner how they feel about house rules. Do you both agree what they are?

7. Have you explained the rules to your child in a calm, patient manner?

8. Who is making the rules in your house? Is it you the adult, or your child within?

9. Are there any points of conflict on which you could shift your ground?

10. Are there any areas where you could allow your child to take the lead?

11. Looking at life from your child's perspective, are there any areas where they could see you as unreasonable?

Rules And Values

All families have rules. You may not even be aware of most of them, but they will exist. Rules usually come from how we believe we should behave. Couples, when they first set up home together, have rules that are unspoken. It is only when, for example, visitors come to stay that they may become conscious that their routine is broken, and things need to be done differently; the rules change. So it is when a baby arrives, the rules change, and the routines are different - and my goodness how different! Life with a child is ever changing and evolving. The rules that are appropriate for the family with one baby will have changed by the time that baby is a teenager with possibly one or more siblings. It is important to acknowledge that the rules we live by are not static. Rules are there to help us live our lives in safety and harmony. They should facilitate our daily routines, not dominate. Most rules are given to children as responses to situations that have arisen or because they have been passed through the generations.

I cannot give you a set of rules to guide you through the child rearing years, but I can help you think through what rules matter to you and your family.

First of all, know why you are insisting on a particular rule. Take the issue of cleanliness as an example. We need to keep our children clean for obvious health reasons, but how clean is clean? Nappies for example need to be changed as often as they are wet or soiled; however, can you tolerate jam or paint stains? Is it easy for you to change your child's clothes? If you went for a walk would you mind other people seeing your child with muddy hands and knees, or would it not bother you? Some parents see it as a sign that their child has been allowed to play in a child-like way, while other parents believe that children need to respect their clothes and should look neat and tidy at all times when they are outside the home. How you feel about it is likely to depend on your current circumstances, how your parents felt, and the beliefs and values they gave to you. Your partner's position as well as yours will also determine how it is handled from your child's point of view. Have you ever discussed it or is it just one of those unwritten rules you both agree on? To save confusion for your child you need to know where you both stand. Having different beliefs just means that you both need to compromise and work out what is acceptable for you in your family. There will be implicit, unspoken rules for all areas of life.

It is best that those involved in your children's care have similar standards and agree on the same rules. Consistency for children, in the areas discussed in this chapter, is important, otherwise confusion arises, and in the next chapter I explain why consistency in behaviour is not always possible. A lack of agreement between parents can offer the opportunity for manipulation by children. This would place them in an unfortunate position because, while they may use an opportunity to manipulate, they would not necessarily be comfortable actually doing it. It is very important that parents discuss these issues before they arise. Where there is disagreement, then a problem-solving approach will be helpful - for example, the method devised by Thomas Gordon and explained in Chapter 7.

Some rules are fairly standard and will be in place in many homes, for example:

* no jumping on the furniture
* no touching electrical sockets or equipment
* no playing with matches or fire
* no writing or drawing on walls or furniture
* we wash every day
* flush the toilet after use
* no ball games inside the house.

The reason for most of the above are safety or cleanliness and there would be little disagreement. Not all rules have a practical or safety basis and it is these that provide a rich ground for disagreement and misunderstanding. It is important that you and your partner know what these rules are, agree them, and then apply them consistently. If you need to change the rules, say so, and explain why. The sort of areas you need to agree on are listed below. It is by no means an exclusive list, I am sure you will know of many more potentially problematic areas that relate to your unique position.

* bedtimes
* table manners
* watching television
* violent games
* what constitutes spoiling
* allowing sweets
* smacking
* general politeness
* cleanliness
* having friends in the house
* tidiness of rooms.

As children grow the areas for rules will change. It is best if these are thought through and discussed rather than imposed arbitrarily or reactively in a hasty way. I discuss some of these in more detail in the following chapters. Parents can tie themselves in knots with rules. For some adults, becoming parents forces them, for the first time, to acknowledge different value systems stemming from those inherited from their own parents. This can cause arguments and disagreements between parents. It can also lead to confusion and division within the family. If disagreements arise between adults over issues then the resolution of those areas of conflict should be done out of hearing of the child concerned. It is very frightening to a child to think that s/he is the cause of an argument between their parents. Of course it is not the child's fault - it will be the parents, and the way the problem is handled. Suggesting that children are the cause of problems in marriage is to give children power they do not merit and to load them with responsibility they do not deserve. Issues may arise because children have thrown light upon them. However, it is the way those issues are dealt with by adults that will determine the outcome. The list above can cause endless arguments between parents, and between parents and their children. If that is happening then each parent needs to stop, take a step back, and say, "Why do I feel so strongly about this? Who told me it was so important? If I make other choices what will happen? How can we move on from here?" When parents do not agree, children learn to play one off against the other to get their own way.

Values

Rules are easy to enforce while children are young. Many of them are absolutely necessary for the safety of our children, but many of them arise because of the beliefs and value systems of their parents. Values can cause a great deal of trouble as children go into the teenage years. When children are very small the majority of them will accept parents' value systems without question. This largely remains the case until they start to look at who they are, their life, and the lives of their parents, and question what they really want. This is one of the hardest stages of development for parents to cope with. It can leave them with damaged relationships that can take years to repair.

Children rarely adopt all their parents' values. Life is constantly evolving. For example, just as words go in and out of use, so do beliefs and values. Those in power at the moment, trying to stultify the English language by trying to make children in all parts of the country pronounce words the same way, are like King Canute who tried to order the tide not to come in. The water kept on coming, and so the spoken word will continue to evolve - otherwise we would all be speaking Anglo-Saxon. Fashions are the same. The evolution of clothing is a slow but relentless process. Yet parents' emotions run high on this subject, and schools make a great deal of work for themselves. When I was at school in the sixties we were in trouble for wearing our skirts too short. Currently, at my elder daughter's school, girls have been in trouble for having their skirts not only too short but also too long. Why do adults become so exercised by teenage fashions? This is not the place to go into the reasons in great detail, but two of the main reasons are values and power.

Adults hold certain beliefs about the attire young people should wear. They usually believe they should dress as they do because it has become the conventional way. Most teenagers will negotiate times to wear what current adult protocol dictates, and times to wear what their peer group approves. Unfortunately some parents are not so yielding and will insist on their young adults adhering to standards acceptable only to them. Some offspring will go along with their parents' wishes and others will not.

Again, an example from my youth to compare with today. The sixties saw the emergence of the Beatles and the Rolling Stones, with a huge influence on boys' hairstyles. Many young men were sent home from school until they had their hair cut because those with power valued the fifties hair style, which was very short. Today, schools are sending boys home because they have too little hair left after a trip to the barbers! The young men of the sixties now hold the power.

A Perennial Problem

If you think of it logically what is the difference between 9.30 pm and 10.30 pm, apart from an hour? Parents and children run into all sorts of problems about the time the children should be home. When it comes down to it the main reason parents want children in at a certain time on a Saturday night is because they believe that, beyond a certain time, their children are more likely to be up to mischief, or they are worried they will get themselves into trouble one way or another. Also, many parents have an illogical belief that they need to control their teenagers' times out of the house. This is based on the parenting model they carry in their heads from their own early days. Parents will give all sorts of reasons for children to be in at a particular time, such as "you need your sleep," or "you have to do so-and-so tomorrow," or they question their children's reliability "what can you possibly be doing after 9.30 pm anyway?" They continually create roadblocks during these confrontations and end up either using power with "well you won't go out at all then," or give up entirely as their teenager slams the door and disappears anyway. The child will probably stay out later to delay the inevitable row when they do return.

Other areas in which you are likely to encounter value collisions will be manners, acceptable tidiness, cleanliness, attitudes towards homework, politics and job goals.

Your children are much more likely to accept your values if they like you and if your relationship with them is good. It comes as something of a shock to some young adults to look back at the turbulent home life and realise that they were responsible for so much rudeness and unreasonable behaviour. On some occasions, even more shocking, can be the realisation that they did not really like their parents very much. They loved them and were grateful to them for providing the basic needs of food, shelter, clothes and parental love but, sadly, when they were old enough to evaluate the situation they were in, they found they did not like many of the things their parents valued and stood for. Indeed, their parents were not the sort of people they would choose to be friendly with!

What to do

Look at the questions devised for you throughout this book and especially at those on rules and values and parenting styles. Look at your values and rules and your parenting style. Which ones can you change if necessary? Which of your child's unacceptable values can you go along with? See how many you can find.

Can you accept that life is constantly evolving and changing? That some of the attitudes held by young people today are there because life for them is different from when you were their age? If you are able to accept that then you are part of the way there.

Listening will help. It will help you to understand your child's point of view. Informative messages are unlikely to have any impact because, when there are disagreements over value issues, the only person likely to be affected is your child. The effect on you, such as embarrassment, is your problem not your child's. They will point this out to you. If you move in with using your power, the older your child is, the more you risk driving them away from you. Younger teenagers will become angry and resentful. It is a very difficult time for them as well. Not only must you accept that some change is inevitable, but that there will be some things you simply cannot change because the risk is too great and the distress of enforcement unnecessary.

Trust

There comes a point in every parent's life when they just have to trust that they have done a good job, the best possible one for their child. They will have to trust that the foundations they laid in their children's lives are strong enough to carry them through life in the outside world. Parents have to trust themselves before they can trust their children.

Giving your child your trust is a valuable gift. If it is genuinely given and the relationship between you is good then it is likely to be as strong a protection for your child's well being as is the stable background you have provided.

Advice for Parents

Rules

1. If at all possible, say "yes" the first time.

2. Have as few imposed rules as possible.

3. Explain rules before they are needed.

4. Explain why, when you need to be inconsistent.

5. Acknowledge that it can be confusing when you need to change the rules.

6. Be prepared to negotiate with your child if s/he sees a need for a change in the rules.

7. Be fair in the way rules operate.

7. Understand yourself and why you are insisting on a certain rule.

Democratic Parent

"We've discussed this. I have explained you can go another time but not this weekend. I'm sorry you feel this way about it but there you are, we all have to compromise sometimes and this time you are."

Laissez-faire Parent

"OK, you win, I'll ring Gran to say we're off to the adventure playground and she can come another time."

Parents' Questions

Chapter 7 - Bad Behaviour

1. Make a list of all the behaviours you believe to be unacceptable.

2. Ask your partner to do the same.

3. Compare the lists
   * Which behaviours are harmful and which are annoying to you both?
   * How many are the same?
   * How many are different?
   * Be sure to discuss the differences.

4. Do you remember a time when you were told you were badly behaved?

5. Was it justified?

6. As a parent would you have handled it differently?

Bad Behaviour

The defining of 'bad' behaviour is a difficult thing to do because it is so subjective and dependent on individuals' beliefs and levels of tolerance. What may be 'bad' behaviour to one parent may not be to another. Behaviour that is considered normal in one household may be totally unacceptable in another. This is not because standards are 'higher' or 'lower', it is because what is important to some people is very different from what is important to others.

My job sometimes involves working with parents when they have difficulty in managing their children at home. Recently, one mother with four children had welcomed my help because she described herself as being "totally unable to control" her daughter at home and then gave me an example of her daughter's disobedience when she refused to eat her crusts at breakfast that morning. "After all," she said, "if she is allowed to leave her crusts, what will I have?" at which she paused, and, very naughtily, I intervened and said "Fat birds in the garden?" (because we put our breakfast scraps out for the birds every day and enjoy watching them come to eat).

The mother blinked at me quite uncomprehendingly, I explained what I did with the uneaten crusts. Clearly, she did not approve. She regarded the eating of all the food on the plate by all her children as essential and undermining of her authority if they failed, and one 'naughty' child leaving crusts behind might well encourage further 'bad' behaviour in the others if she allowed it to continue. This mother was an authoritarian type of parent and would be in for more mutinies in the future.

I hope the above illustrates the dilemma of defining 'bad' behaviour. In this chapter I am not talking about criminal behaviour but the sort of behaviours parents would deal with when children have crossed the bounds of acceptability within the home. In many respects the defining of bad behaviour is rather like deciding on what the rules should be in a household. Parents need to ask themselves some questions first such as:

* can you agree on what 'bad' behaviour is?
* can you always be consistent in your demands about particular behaviours?
* do your notions of 'good' and 'bad' behaviour fit in with the rest of your family?
* do your notions of 'good' and 'bad' behaviour fit in with the rest of society?
* do you realise that you will have to change your understanding of 'good' and 'bad' behaviour with the age of your child, the time and place?

Below, I discuss those questions and hope to help you think about what behaviours will be acceptable to you.

As parents, can you agree?

Do you have to agree about all things at all times? In the course of your child's eighteen years it is very unlikely that you will be able to agree on everything to do with behaviour. Even if you both have similar backgrounds you will have experienced life differently in your separate families and therefore there will, at the very least, be small differences in beliefs about behaviour. I would like to emphasise the word differences. Difficulties that arise about behaviour, dress codes, etc. are usually to do with the perceptions and beliefs that make up people's value systems. There are often no definitive rights and wrongs in situations, just differences. In trying to agree about bad behaviour or to make a decision it is worth asking some questions such as:

* Will the child be harmed?
* Will another person be harmed?
* Will property be harmed?

If the answers to these questions are "No," then maybe the behaviour offends one or both of you without causing harm.

As children become more mature they can be supported to understand that parents have some different values between them and that the process of becoming an adult involves establishing one's own value system.

Consistency

There is a myth that parents need to be consistent at all times, this is not true. Some consistency is necessary some of the time as discussed in the last chapter. Too much consistency can lead to unnecessary rigidity and is favoured by those who tend towards too much authoritarianism. Thomas Gordon dispels the notion of consistency when he says his P.E.T. (Parent Effectiveness Training) model will *"help parents understand how they inevitably will be inconsistent"*. He continues *"In P.E.T. classes we first ask parents to visualise a rectangle or window in front of them, through which they see all the behaviours of their child. Then we show how every parent's rectangle contains two different kinds of behaviour, and that the same behaviour can be placed into either category at different times.*

acceptable	Pounding on the piano when mother is rested and busy.
and	
unacceptable.	Pounding on the piano when mother is tired and napping.

When a parent is feeling rested and is busy doing something interesting and satisfying, her three year old daughter's pounding on a piano might be quite acceptable to her. Yet the same behaviour would be unacceptable if mother were tired and trying to take a nap. Furthermore, there are days when a parent's Area of Acceptance is very large - everything is going well and almost nothing perturbs him. His rectangle would look like this:

Many acceptable behaviours

and

Few unacceptable behaviours

If at another time that father is upset or worried, everything seems to be going wrong, his rectangle might very well look like this!

Few acceptable behaviours

and

Many unacceptable behaviours

On such a day, almost anything his child might do would feel unacceptable to him... When parents understand that, after all, they are only human beings with their own changing moods, then they can become more able to live with their fluctuating feelings toward their children, dropping the heavy burden of guilt their inconsistent behaviour had produced.

Gordon goes on to explain that there are other reasons for parents' inconsistencies. One is the nature of the personality of the child, and the other is environmental. As a teacher I have often been aware of how some children provoke adults to push them away, for example, the noisy, boisterous, cheeky child is often less appealing than the normally obedient, quiet child. If both children accidentally spill paint, then the adult's reaction to those two is likely to be different. The very active child is likely to encounter irritation and blame, whereas the second child, who is 'normally good', will more likely encounter greater tolerance when she has an accident.

The environment is also an influence on what behaviour we will accept. Gordon gives us an example: *"Take rowdy horseplay. Outside in the yard, it may be quite acceptable to Dad - in fact even enjoyable. In the living room, most of the same behaviours will be unacceptable."*

Thus our levels of acceptance vary, Gordon calls it the "principle of inconsistency." I have to agree with him when he says *"you will inevitably be inconsistent from day to day, with your different moods, with different children and in different environments. Accept this principle and you will eliminate a lot of guilt and anxiety."*

He also says that the "united front" is unnecessary, *"these kinds of conflicts that so easily erode marriage relationships."* He believes that partners fall into the trap of acting as 'agents' for one another, usually mothers for fathers, when they really do not agree with what they are saying or doing. Gordon advises individual parents to be true to their own instincts. For example, one parent may be upset by an untidy bedroom which does not concern the other. In that case the tidy parent will strongly negotiate to ensure his needs are met because perhaps he is responsible for the vacuuming. The other might explain, "It does not bother me but it is important to your father."

The Wider Context

No family unit is an island. We all have to deal with the outside world. We have relatives and friends. Our children go to school. They have their peer group and teachers to contend with. We have workplace colleagues. All these people will hold their own views and beliefs about 'bad' behaviour, or what is and is not acceptable. They may influence your views. You may want to adopt some of their ideas, or you may so disagree with them that you choose to do quite the opposite. Whatever your views, other people are likely to be in a position to comment on your child's behaviour or possibly to be looking after your child for periods of time. For example, grandparents may baby-sit, nursery school helpers will be looking after your child, and so on. Therefore, what you do and think and the demands you make on your child will depend, quite possibly, on who else is involved, and how they influence you. If your child were to spend a day with its grandparents, then the instructions you would give and the way you would expect them to behave might be quite different if your child were to be spending the day with a group of friends. Thus our demands and expectations change with the circumstances. Most children understand that and are willing to accept the differences.

Age

Age will also make a difference to what you perceive as being 'bad' behaviour. For example, a child smearing yoghurt all over its plate at the age of twelve months might be considered cute. At two years you will be trying to explain that the yoghurt goes on the spoon and into the mouth. The same activity at five or six years is likely to earn a rebuke with a demand that it is cleared up.

The way you respond to individual children will depend on their age. That will evoke in older or younger brothers and sisters the cry "its not fair, s/he gets away with it, why can't I?" Differentiated bed times causes this type of cry in our house. As I have already indicated, it is quite legitimate to make different behavioural demands as needs arise, but be honest. You must acknowledge that you are being inconsistent and explain why. It will be

OK, your children will be getting a good role model. You will be modelling:

* An understanding of what you are doing
* Honesty
* Being informational
* Being in control

Bad behaviour is sometimes a subjective observation made according to the circumstance and individual's interpretation. Whatever you decide, if you are indicating to the child that you are unhappy with your child's behaviour, remember it is only the behaviour that is unacceptable, never, ever the child. You must always phrase your disapproval to make that quite clear.

A.B.C.

A.B.C. stands for Antecedents, Behaviour and Consequences. It is a model used to explain a structured way of managing children's behaviour, and it can, in some limited circumstances, be very useful.

Antecedents means what happens before the behaviour takes place. As a parent trying to regulate the behaviour of a child who is giving cause for concern it may be helpful for you to understand what happens immediately before particular behaviours. Is there a regular pattern to trigger certain unacceptable behaviours? Some parents can identify the consumption of certain things such as a cola drink or sweets with particular E numbers in them. Other parents can identify household events that will cause problem behaviours. If you can pinpoint a particular thing that always precedes certain 'bad' behaviour then you will be in a strong position to do something about it.

It can be important that children know that their behaviour will invoke certain consequences. They need to know this in advance. They need to be told that, should a certain behaviour happen, then certain consequences will follow. For this to be successful then you must follow through. Therefore, it is necessary that you give consequences that are realistic for all of you. For example, if you say to your child that they must be in by a certain time and they are not, it would be reasonable to let her off the first time. However, on the second occasion it would be useful to point out that if they fail to arrive home on time then there will be consequences. The punishment must be 'fair' in that it reflects the crime, so a fair punishment might be staying in the next time for one night. If the punishment is seen to be unfair because it goes on for too long, or is seen as disproportionate to the crime, then the child becomes resentful and angry and more inclined to rebel. See Chapters 6 and 8 on rules and punishments.

The A.B.C. model will only work if you as a parent explains very carefully before the behaviour has happened that should it happen then there will be consequences, and you make quite sure that the consequences do take place!

Advice for Parents

Bad Behaviour

1. Always disapprove of the behaviour, never the child.

2. Be true to yourself: do you really find the behaviour unacceptable or are you responding to someone else's view?

3. If it is harmful then you need to stop it.

4. If it is annoying, say so and either remove yourself, or ask your child to stop or go to another room.

5. Remember, what is considered bad in your house may be acceptable elsewhere, so consider, is it really bad?

Parents' Questions

Chapter 8 - Discipline and Punishment

This section is intended to stimulate thoughts about your beliefs concerning punishments and examine how you use punishment, if you use it at all.

1. Is punishment a necessary part of child rearing?

2. Were you punished as a child?

3. Do punishments have to be big to make an impact?

4. Should they be used regularly?

5. Are punishments always tangible?

6. Were you fairly punished as a child?

7. What punishments do you use in your home?

8. Who gets punished in your home?

9. If you get things wrong, fail to do something, or some other misdemeanour, who punishes you?

Discipline and Punishment

We are constantly being told by the media that children lack discipline. What precisely does that mean - what is discipline? When I ask parents I am given a variety of answers. Essentially it seems to mean, to most parents, punishment. Yet we talk about wanting our children to have self-discipline.

There is much confusion over what constitutes discipline, but a certain knowledge that children need a great deal of it and it isn't very nice for them. I would suggest that a large part of the problem for many children and their parents is that there is just too much discipline in the form of punishment in families, without the strategies that encourage self-discipline. This can lead to children feeling distanced from their parents, afraid to confide in them, and alienated in their teenage years. This chapter will discuss the value of punishment and suggest alternatives to it that will encourage self-discipline.

When young children are traumatised by punishment, physical smacking, isolation from the family, and so on, they are usually confused by it. In most cases they are unlikely to fully understand what is going on - how can they when in reality the parents fail to understand. Children are subjected to repeated traumas. They become used to them. They internalise the fact that it must be good for them:

* because their parents say so - and a child will believe them
* because their parents have identified such badness in them.

Their self-image becomes one of "I am bad, I am unloveable."

Many children fall foul of adults for any number of reasons, for example because they have not listened, understood, forgotten, or misinterpreted something. I have often been horrified to see tiny tots of no more than eighteen months hauled off from some inappropriate activity, being smacked and shouted at. The bewildered child cries, but does not make the connection between his behaviour and the sudden attack from the mother or adult looking after them.

Children are egocentric beings, intent on having their own needs met, they often live in their own little worlds. Misbehaviour is only very rarely deliberate, and in those cases where it is deliberate it usually begins as sheer mischieviousness without understanding the consequences. Otherwise there is likely to be a definite problem in the relationship that needs resolving.

Over the years that I have worked with damaged children, their parents and teachers, I have often been struck by how dogmatically the adults cling to the belief in the value of punishment. When it is clearly not working, punishment is often justified by saying something along the lines of "it may not be doing him any good, but I have to make an example of him." Even the most humane and intelligent of adults will trot out such rubbish.

Adults cling to the value of punishment because it was something that was done to them. I can remember wanting to hit my first child and thinking why do I feel such a strong urge to hurt this helpless little thing that I love so much? It was then that I started on my quest to understand what I needed to do to be an effective, as well as a loving, parent, because I knew I could not inflict on my child what had been done to me in the name of good practice. Punishing, certainly hitting, children is not good practice and never was.

The reason we cling to punishment as good is that when we are young and defenceless we have to accept all that is done to us is for our own good, and we believe it without question. To survive we need to identify with and love our parents unconditionally. The home we live in is the only home we know, we have no opportunity to compare and contrast others. Anyway, to a defenceless child what use is it to be able to do that? The model of a parent that our parents give us is the one that becomes our bedrock, our point of reference. The model our parents give us is usually one that has been passed down through the generations with very little alteration.

To a defenceless child the physical size of a parent makes them powerful, let alone the fact that they control whether they eat, have shelter and clothes. Parents hold all the power. Children identify with them. They internalise all that the parents are and stand for. They may appear to rebel against this in their teenage years, but the fact remains that what a child lives with in the early years will form their internal working model. They are likely to repeat the pattern of hurt and pain. Indeed, when a parent is hurting its own child it may well be experiencing a sort of cathartic release for the pain and humiliation it experienced.

For many people damage was done at an early age. They have forgotten what it felt like to experience punishment, and it has been buried by fear, love, time or justifications for the parents' behaviour. They then fail to see what they are doing to their own children. They are so convinced by their faulty internal model that what they are doing is right, they are unable to recognise the pain and humiliation in the eyes of their children.

Alice Miller (1987, 1987b) likens it to a prisoner being tortured. They are traumatised and because there is no escape they come to identify with their captors. What escape is there for children when they are in unhappy or cruel homes? They have to identify with their parents and learn to accept what comes their way. Without insight they are likely to just repeat the pattern.

Boundaries

Limits need to be set for young children. There will, of course, be times when they will test them. The purpose of a limit is to act as a safe boundary beyond which a child should not go. It is up to the parent to be sure that the boundary is secure.

Some limits will need to be set for safety, health or some other practical reason. Some will be set for the parents' own convenience or emotional needs. Children will accept your discipline and the fact that you have needs. However, you should know what they are and be able to explain them to your child simply, clearly and patiently. You should also explain what the limits are before the children are close to them, preferably finding a time when it is possible to be quiet, calm and reflective (see Chapter 6 on Rules). The rules you establish within your family should be facilitative, they should help you work together. These rules will change as your needs change. They are best established by negotiation, taking everyone's needs into account.

What do we mean by discipline?

Children's understanding of morality, of right from wrong, comes from their parents. Parents are the earliest role models. Later in life they will have other role models such as friends and teachers, but to start with a child's first experience of right and wrong is at home. Hitting and smacking is not good discipline. Nor is yelling and shouting. Discipline needs to come from within and the best way to help children to be well disciplined is to treat them with respect. Parents are advised to respect the fact that they are dealing with children whose understanding of the world has yet to mature. Empathic tolerance needs to be shown for the child's feelings and emotional life. It is very hard for a child to live in the adult world and is especially so when the adults have long forgotten how embarrassing, confusing and difficult it can be to try to make sense of complex social rules, long words and so on. If children never experience the love, tolerance and respect they need, how on earth can they grow into adults with those qualities? The best form of discipline comes in a form that helps to develop internal controls, and that does not come from externally applied punishments. As a parent you should be looking to have a co-operative relationship with your child rather than unquestioning obedience. We train our dogs to be obedient. For our children we want to encourage thought, creativity, flexibility and the willingness to be responsibly co-operative with us in family life.

Punishment

Punishment means that an offender is made to suffer for an offence. Are some of the punishments allotted to children really what is needed when they have got things wrong? Do punishments show children the way forward? How to avoid offending again? How to get it right next time? Severe punishments such as physical beatings, deprivations and humiliations cause far more problems. They can:

* damage a child's self-esteem
* actually encourage them to lie to avoid being punished (adults do this all the time)
* damage and stunt creativity, by discouraging them from trying or taking risks because if they get it wrong they will be punished
* emphasise, rather than minimise, bad behaviour

* encourage bad behaviour rather than stop it
* put parents into an inappropriate role model using an inappropriate agent to control
* show children by example that it is acceptable grown up behaviour for bigger, stronger people to cause pain to smaller, weaker people
* cause long-term psychological damage
* permanently damage your relationship with your child because of anger and resentment
* damage your child's ability to be an effective parent
* ensure that inappropriate punishments continue into the next generation.

An eighty-two year old told me one day of the hurt and resentment she still felt remembering a time when her mother beat her brother with a stick for something. She claimed never to have felt the same again about her mother after the incident.

If you feel you have to resort to punishing your child, use any punishment sparingly. Always use the absolute minimum and of the shortest duration possible. I have encountered parents who have prevented a six year old from watching television for a week. This is far too long, one night would be ample. If a child is uncertain if it is morning or afternoon, if they cannot remember whether the next meal is lunch or tea, then prolonged punishments are of no value at all. They constantly remind the child that she is "bad" and highlight the misdeed that has probably been forgotten.

Always use alternatives to punishment first. Make sure you praise and encourage the behaviour you want. With very young children you can often simply divert their attention onto something else. Be explicit about what you want. Remind the child of rules before they need to use them - especially if they are for the child's safety. Explain why you are unhappy. Try to elicit your child's viewpoint, they may have done something "naughty" to punish you or a sibling for some perceived hurt, but do not harangue with questions. Very often they simply do not know why. Were you always able to explain when you were a child?

Reparation gives children the chance to repair some of the damage they may feel they have done. Often they just want the chance to put it right. Punishments prevent that. Discuss with your child how she thinks she could make amends? You are likely to find she will have some very appropriate ideas. Put physical punishments so far down your list that they fall off! Try instead this two stage approach:

Stage 1

* discussion about the problem
* negotiation
* reparation
* problem solving (see Chapter 7).

Stage 2

Negotiate any punishment. Ask your child what they think should happen. You will probably find that their idea of what punishment they should receive will far exceed any thing you had in mind. This will give you the opportunity to say "you are not that bad therefore I don't have to punish you that hard." Make the punishment as small as possible. I can remember hearing a radio interview with a man who had been to prison for the first time. He said that when he first went into goal he thought it was a dreadful place that he would never survive. Had he been released within the first month he would have continued in that belief. However, as the months went on, he became used to the environment. He felt that the prolonged punishment had blunted the threat of that punishment for him in the future. He left prison believing that if he had survived that experience he could survive anything. Children are the same, if the punishment tariff is too high too early they become immune to it, (see Unpunishable Children below). Try the following if you still feel punishment is necessary:

* sending your child to their room for 15 minutes
* no computer for an evening
* missing a television programme, just one for the first few times
* having only half pocket money
* missing out on one of their magazines for one week
* not allowing them out to play for an hour
* making them come in early.

Always give your child the chance to put things right and to make amends in a genuine way. By that I mean a way that is right for the child, and not imposed by you which could do further damage. For example, an enforced apology can just store up anger and resentment, it can cause further confrontation and escalate the situation. Just think about it for a moment. Can you apologise to someone if you are still feeling angry and resentful? Why then should you expect a child to be able to apologise unconditionally if he or she is still feeling angry? We often demand a greater level of maturity from our children than we are capable of ourselves. Try always to say something warm and positive as soon as possible afterwards, and find something to help maintain self-esteem.

Who are you punishing?

Some parents issue a punishment without thinking through the consequences for themselves and the rest of the family. If you like to use punishment then when you do punish your child you must decide on a punishment that suits you. Take the example of keeping a child in for a week without television. What is a child, used only to amusing itself through the television, going to do for a week? Parents often end up suffering themselves or abandoning the punishment.

Look at the list above. If you are using punishments give a warning, for example "If you do ... then I will do..." Make them manageable for you all and of short duration. This way, at least, your child will learn that you mean what you say, and will not have the added problem of your failure to follow through.

Unpunishable Children - A Warning

Some children are so punished that punishment has no effect. They become unpunishable children. Two researchers, Davies and Maliphant (in Maines and Robinson (1991), have measured children's physiological responses to being in trouble and found that some children do not have the usual responses. Examples of physiological responses to situations are an increase in heart beat, sweating, dry mouth and trembling hands. All or just one of these may occur in stressful situations.

Anticipation of threat and actual punishment should produce a physiological response of one sort or another. Some children simply do not react at all. They can seem not to care less. Their bodies seem to shut down. They can pretend the punishment is not happening to them, allow punishment to take place and then carry on as normal. This reaction to punishment increases the adult's frustration and is likely to spur the adult on to inflicting more and more severe punishments with less and less effect. The amount of research in this area is very small but it does indicate that too much punishment at an early age can have the effect of switching children off.

You will also find that all "hard core" prisoners experienced severe punishment when very young. The punishment that could be given by teachers and the authorities meant nothing by comparison. Their true selves had been so damaged and traumatised at a very early age that, without prolonged psychological help, they became untouchable by later punishment.

Every time I talk to groups of teachers they can always recognise one or two such youngsters who appear outside the head's office day after day. What trouble we, as a society, store up for ourselves because of our love affair with punishment.

Smacking

Because we are so enamoured of smacking and therefore it is widely used, I have devoted a complete chapter to it. I would like to say it is demeaning to you in so far as it devalues both you and your child. Try everything else first, such as:

   * ignoring
   * setting rules
   * praise
   * rewards.
   * problem solving

* modelling
* information messages.

All these are described in detail in the book, see the index to find the relevant pages.

Use Love

Punishment is not a good way of helping your child to get things right in the future. Only the people who hold power over others are able to punish. Bigger, stronger people can physically punish smaller and weaker people but not vice versa. Punishment is about power and control. It used to be thought correct to physically punish servants and workers for misdeeds. That is no longer acceptable to society, yet it remains with us that we should inflict physical and psychological pain on our children when they get something wrong; and that we must not give them too much praise lest they become big headed. The belief that condemnation is good and encouragement is to be used sparingly is one of the great ills of our society. It is a great disservice that we do to the tender developing psyche of our young. Love is good, unconditional love and acceptance is the best sort, and should be expressed through hugs and kind looks whenever possible. Children who are loved in this way will feel good. They will want to please the adults that love them this way. If they get something wrong and it is pointed out to them in an informational and loving way, then they will want to put it right as quickly as possible.

Some More Strategies

Problem Solving

The psychologist Dr Thomas Gorton created a very useful framework for the problem solving process in a series of six steps. They are:

* Step 1 - The problem is defined by need
* Step 2 - Lots of solutions are produced (brainstorm)
* Step 3 - The potential merit of each solution is appraised
* Step 4 - Plan who is to do what, where, when
* Step 5 - Carry out the plan
* Step 6 - Review the plan and the process.

Step 1 - The problem defined by need.
The first step is the foundation process, which I liken to the foundations of a building. If the foundations are unstable, the building will develop cracks and fall apart. So too will Stages 4 and 5 (if you get that far) if the problem has not been accurately defined.

Many people, children in particular, find it difficult to state their needs clearly. This will be especially difficult if you are attempting this process just from reading this book and you have not been in a habit of allowing your child to state his/her needs. You will need to bring the vital skill of listening to this process. You will have to follow the three stages of listening, see Chapter 15 for details of this. You will have to think carefully and tune into what the real need is. Very often I find that parents of older children dress up all sorts of excuses as needs, when really the problem is that the child is asking to do something that conflicts with the parents' value system. Remember the example of the teenager who wanted to stay out beyond a certain time? The parents' need to know could have been because of anxiety over the child's safety, or simply the wish to control the young adult's behaviour.

I will explain the working of the process through the example of two parents, Sue and James, and their son Ian. It was a case of Ian needing to exert some independence for himself at age seventeen and of his parents being able to let go and to learn to be less anxious and protective (or possessive, as Ian saw it).

Sue and James could not sleep until they knew Ian was home safely, they both had to be up to work in the mornings so they needed their sleep. Ian wished to establish a social life free from mum and dad nagging, he was seventeen after all!

The family eventually used the process and found it very helpful. The needs were:

* sleep for the parents
* independence for the child.

This stage of the process will probably take the longest because it is when parents are most likely to put in place effective barriers to communication. Also, neither side may identify what their needs are accurately, or explain them assertively.

Step 2 - Producing solutions

The idea of this stage is to generate, but not evaluate or judge in any way, as many solutions as possible. Use a piece of paper.

In the example above the family generated some of the following solutions, that Ian should:

* stay home on week nights
* give phone number of every contact to parents
* leave home
* carry a bleeper or a mobile phone
* father or mother to drop Ian off and collect him for all outings
* agree a time to be home, ring if unavoidably detained.

Can you guess which solutions were produced by Ian and which by his parents?

All suggestions, however fantastic or unrealistic, go down on paper. This process is called brainstorming. Big business uses it amongst workers and executives for such things as to enhance work practices, generate new produce ideas and marketing ideas. Not only can it be fun, but also it is very useful.

Step 3 - Appraise the potential merit of each solution

Ian's suggestion that he should leave home was discarded very quickly, as neither he nor his parents wanted that solution. His suggestion that he carry a bleeper was facetious, although his mother did wonder if a mobile phone might be a good idea in case he needed to ring in an emergency. Ian and his father rejected that, but both for different reasons. They eventually agreed a solution. The process they should have gone through at this stage was:

1. Each family member was asked which solution was preferred.
2. Which was their second choice.
3. They then saw how much agreement there was, how many solutions were the same.
4. Being assertive about their own needs to reach a consensus.

It is best not to dwell on the negative choices because:

* it is time consuming
* it can throw up roadblocks
* it is not relevant to finding a positive solution.

Note: Consensus is essential to achieving a situation where everyone wins. You are avoiding having a loser with this plan.

Step 4 - Plan who is to do what, where, when.

The solution they all accepted was that, on weekdays, Ian would state at what time he was coming home. If he was going to be any later he would ring before he was due home to say what was happening. For their part, his parents would not give him the third degree on the phone if he had to ring home, and they would trust him. In trusting him, if he was later than planned and they needed to go to bed, they could go to sleep. If they did not achieve sleep, that was their problem, not Ian's. They set a date to review the plan.

Step 5 - Carry out the plan.

Trust between Ian and his parents had become a little fragile, so he decided to test the plan at the earliest opportunity. To his surprise his parents did not nag him at all the next morning - instead they thanked him for keeping to the plan! Trust has become stronger between this family, and the plan worked.

Step 6 - Review the plan and the process.
If at all possible review the process immediately or very soon afterwards. Give yourself enough time to see if the plan has worked and then review it some time later. If the plan has not worked, the two most likely reasons are:

* the problem was not accurately defined
* someone's needs were not met

There is no point in deteriorating into blaming and other roadblocks. Re-examine the problem, and start the process again. Listen very carefully; encourage an assertive, needs-led response.

If the process has been followed, all parties have assertively explained their problems, and their needs have been met, then there is a high probability that the new arrangements will work. The likelihood of success is even greater if there is already good-will emanating from a strong, loving relationship.

Giving Informational Messages

When we tell children off we usually do it in such a way that we blame and itemise the behaviour. Seldom do we explain why we feel as we do and we almost never explain the effect it has on us. The reason we moan at our children or tell them off is because we want them to stop and change their behaviour. Unfortunately, our reaction to what has gone wrong does little more than draw their attention to our displeasure and make them feel ashamed or guilty, neither are positive feelings that will encourage change. The traditional "telling off" that leads to anger, resentment or guilt does not point the way to change. It is for us as parents to use language more effectively. One way of doing this is to use what has been called assertive messages or "I" messages that are informational. Such a message has three component parts:

* **Behaviour** - you say what you see happening
* **Effect** - say what effect it has on you
* **Feeling** - say how it makes you feel.

An informational message always has three parts and it always starts with the behaviour. You can switch around the feeling and effect, but it is important that you have all three components. It is the perfect tool for the democratic parent. It is assertive and powerful without using power.

Examples of informational messages:

Behaviour	*When you bounce on the furniture*
Feeling	*I find it upsetting*
Effect	*because you will damage the springs and ruin it*

Behaviour	*When I see the towels left on the bathroom floor*
Effect	*I have to pick them up*
Feeling	*and I feel cross about having to do it.*

The most important aspect of an informational message is that the correct feeling is identified by the parent. For example, many parents confuse fear and anger. If their little ones are putting themselves in danger, the parents' reaction is anger driven by fear. It often takes a while to get in touch with genuine emotion, but it is essential for the message to be authentic and therefore ring true with the child being asked to change its behaviour.

An informational message of this sort may or may not make your child feel inclined to alter its behaviour. The quality of your relationship will be important here. If you have a good relationship, the chances are that you regularly listen to your child. It is then likely that your child is also a good listener, it will be a skill they have learned from you. The better your relationship and the more you are both used to listening to each other, the more chance there is that your child will listen to your message.

There is the human factor to consider here. Although messages presented in this way have a high degree of success, make sure you are both calm. You will not give a good informational message if you are in an emotional state. Your child will not be able to listen. Sometimes your child simply may not want to respond, perhaps because it is inconvenient, or he or she does not know how to change, or there is some other reason.

When this happens you have to listen to the response (see Listening). Use the problem solver. You will not however be able to problem solve until you have discovered what the problem is.

Where the basic relationship is good there will be a willingness to please on both sides. With the combination of listening and an informational message there is a high probability of change to more acceptable behaviour, with a decrease in the unacceptable behaviour that is likely to be permanent.

Allow time for new information to sink in. It may take a day or two. If you go back to insisting on immediate obedience you will have wasted your efforts above. Let your child digest what you have said, it usually works better that way.

Advice for Parents

Punishments

1. Use the minimum.

2. Never use sarcasm or humiliation.

3. Negotiate what is "fair" with your child.

4. Never delay punishment.

5. Protect self-esteem for example by finding something nice to say to your child.

6. Make the punishment immediate and of short duration.

7. Explain that you are punishing the deed and not the child.

8. Check that what you are saying and doing is understood.

9. Ask yourself how your child will avoid another punishment next time.

10. Problem solve.

11. Use informational 'I' messages.

12. Is it the adult or child in you wanting to punish, and who are you wanting to punish?

Parents' Questions

Chapter 9 - Smacking

Try to answer these questions honestly. Think back to when you were a small child. Remember the time when you stood waist high to a group of adults.

Ask yourself:

1. Were you smacked as a child?

2. If so what emotions did it evoke in you?

3. Did it help you to understand exactly what you had done wrong or were you sometimes confused?

4. Will smacking your child really help you to develop that resourceful, loving, thinking little person you ultimately want?

5. When do you smack your child - what happens before, what happens after?

6. Is it effective, in other words does it stop your child from ever doing it again and teach them how to get it right next time?

7. How do you feel after you have smacked your child?

8. Was it worthwhile and has it improved your relationship with your child?

Smacking

Smacking is a frequent punishment for children in our society so although there is a chapter on punishment, I have chosen to discuss it on its own because I believe it is different from many other punishments and therefore deserves separate consideration.

Our cultural heritage

Within our society we have conflicting views about when it is and is not acceptable for one human being to hit another. It is, for example, considered wrong for one adult to hit another, even a "slap". We do not allow children to hit one another. Yet smacking, walloping, hitting - all of which are names for physical violence - continue to be considered good practice when adults do it to children. Why?

I believe we have to examine our historical and cultural roots to find the answer. The strong and the powerful have traditionally behaved rather badly towards the weak and less powerful. If we look back to the days when rich people had servants, living and working in their homes, it was accepted practice to physically abuse them. It is not now acceptable practice to physically abuse adult workers for their mistakes. However, it has remained with us as a good thing to do to children.

Brutality has pervaded child rearing throughout British history. It was endemic in schools and reflected practices generally considered acceptable. Jonathan Gathorne-Hardy's (1977) book on public schools documents the life in these places and enables us to glimpse how children suffered. He says that the treatment of children in schools reflected their treatment in wider society. He quotes Burn's Justice of the Peace in the late 18th century (page 39-40) *"Where a schoolmaster, in correcting his scholar, happens to occasion his death ..."* indicating that it was not unknown for teachers to flog children so brutally that it caused death.

Beating children in school became less frequent during the last century and into this, when in 1986 corporal punishment was abolished in state schools. Those in favour of beating children were sure we would see children rioting in the streets in no time at all. Forgetting of course the riots that took place in the past such as the one (of many) noted by Gathorne-Hardy in 1805 (page 57) when,

> *"Led by Byron, the boys dragged the headmaster's desk into the middle of the school and burnt it. They then planned to blow the place up, and actually got as far as laying a trail of gunpowder down a passage ..."*

Literature is littered with stories of badly treated children. Probably the most famous is Dickens. He portrayed a society that appeared to regard young humans as morally bankrupt and incapable of good behaviour unless it was beaten into them. These days we are less inclined towards hitting our children. Although Peter Newell's (1989) work makes sober reading and it is possible to understand why so many people still hit their children. It is because they hold in their heads a model of a parent who hits children at given times.

This has been handed down to us over hundreds of years and countless generations. The vast majority of today's parents are unlikely to go in for the flogging and beating described above, but I do encounter in my work enough children physically damaged by their parents to know that more than an occasional smack on children's legs goes on in too many homes. There is still a great deal of hitting and physical violence that is regarded as good parenting.

> *Recently an eight year old boy explained to me how, when his parents went to bingo, he was left to look after his younger sister and he had to hit her when she was naughty. When I said I disagreed with him about that, he looked at me wide-eyed and reassured me that it was "necessary to teach her right". His mum and dad hit him and how else was he to keep his sister on the straight and narrow?*

We may see fewer broken bones and bruising of children's skin, but there appears to be no lessening of the pain and psychological damage that is not so easy to spot but manifests in the sort of problems listed below.

According to Newell, over 90% of adults in this country have been smacked by their parents. I am not going to condemn today's parents who believe that smacking is acceptable, but I suggest that their beliefs are based on faulty thinking. Of the parent population in this country around 90% will resort to hitting their children at some time during their childhood. Alarmingly about 63% of mothers hit their babies. There does appear to be a change in how people view hitting their children.

Many parents express guilt and regret after resorting to smacking. Parents are more likely to hit when they are tired, stressed, or just fed up and in need of a change of company. In spite of expressions of guilt at resorting to smacking, 75% of those parents who do smack believe that it has some merit and will benefit their children.

Whilst causality cannot be definitely established, frequent and severe physical punishment in childhood has been found to be associated with severe adult deviance, sexual and violent crime, psychaitric disorder and poor maintenance of relationships.

Nowhere can I find any research to suggest that severe physical punishment is good and works. Alice Miller's (1987b) book "For your own good: The roots of violence in childhood" looks at how a brutal early life can affect adult behaviour. We see that she believes that had Adolph Hitler been treated with a little love and kindness he would not have been the leader he proved to be. He was able to be so brutal with the permission of a population who themselves had been treated with similar brutality and humiliation as young children. She says we

> *"continue to infect the next generation with the virus of poisonous pedagogy as long as we claim this kind of upbringing is harmless ... When people who have been beaten or spanked as children attempt to play down the consequences by setting themselves up as examples, even claiming it was good for them, they are inevitably contributing to the continuance of cruelty in the world by this refusal to take their childhood tragedies seriously. Taking over this attitude, their children, pupils and students will in turn beat their own children, citing their parents, teachers and professors as authorities."*

Everywhere in the literature about deviant criminals and murderers one finds those who have been neglected, brutalised or in some way mistreated when as powerless children they struggled to survive and make sense of the confusion, evil and violence that happened to them during their formative years.

Unhelpful

Young children love their parents unconditionally with a great deal of tolerance and acceptance, yet that quality of love is not always reciprocated. The very parent who has hit and hurt the child is likely to be one the child has to turn to for comfort.

The older a child is the more likely she is to remember the humiliation of the experience. This is potentially very damaging for a child's self-esteem, and likely to leave feelings of resentment or anger, particularly if the punishment was perceived as unjust in any way.

Smacking is deeply ingrained in our society as something a "good" parent does in order to ensure a child will become well behaved and moral, simply because so many of us carry in our heads either a model of an authoritarian parent who hit us when we were young, or a hurt, resentful child angry at what was done to us. It does not work, but it does perpetuate the cycle. All I can say is, try not to smack, and never in anger. Be aware of the damage you can do to tender young psyches and bodies.

A parent who believes in smacking a child as a valid way of controlling it or making it comply with the demands or wishes of an adult certainly risks confusing and damaging a very young child . Particularly one who does not have the language to say "Why did you do that?" A smack without any explanation at all is no more than an assault. Parents who rely on smacking are really storing up trouble for themselves. This authoritarian stance will engender anger and resentment and acts against the development of a more mature realtionship in which influence and trust pervade.

Parents are Role Models

A role model is someone we copy, consciously or unconsciously. However with parents we emulate their behaviour because we absorb it at such a young age that it becomes an intimate part of our own subconscious. I have seen many teenagers quite sure they will never ever behave as their parents, only to become almost exact copies in adult life. Children's strategies for coping with difficulties in life and their understanding of how to behave will be developed first at home then later modified and influenced by friends and teachers.

Smacking children conveys the message that it is acceptable and grown up behaviour for big people to hurt small people, and it is acceptable for adults to hurt children to force them to do as they are told. Also if parents lash out at their children when they are angry or tired, the children are given a clear message about how to conduct themselves under such conditions.

If we are trying to encourage patience, tolerance and high self-worth but model the exact opposite, then our words will fall on deaf ears because our children are far more influenced by the way we ourselves behave and the things we do than the words of advice we give them. All the time our children are watching us and learning from us. Much of that learning is subconscious. Our every day behaviour models what is grown up behaviour to our children.

The very best method of prevention is to create an environment and develop a loving relationship whereby your child does not feel the need to be "naughty" or finds it difficult to draw your wrath to such an extent that you want to be physically violent. Where the relationship is normal, I promise you children seek only your love and approval. They have no wish to anger, upset or disappoint you, but when we are learning in any new job or environment, mistakes are made frequently and learning how to get it right when you are a child is no exception.

A good quality loving relationship is the best antidote to the need for punishment, and that includes smacking.

Advice for Parents

Smacking

Hitting children does not show them how to get things right. You may think it punishes something they have got wrong. Smacking is only something a bigger and more powerful person can do to a smaller weaker person. Always try alternatives first, such as:

Stage 1

* ignoring
* setting rules
* using "I" messages
* removing your child
* showing and expressing disapproval.

See Punishments for more explanation of the above strategies.

Stage 2

The ideas below are punishments. Wherever possible negotiate with your child the punishment. always keep them short, always explain why you are giving them.

* loss of television
* loss of one week's pocket money
* staying in for one or two nights after school
* stopping a favourite activity for one night.

Remember: smacking is your choice of punishment - your child did not make you do it - though the child within you may have.

Parents' Questions

Chapter 10 - Serious Misbehaviour

This chapter is only for you if you think you have a really serious problem with your child. Be sure you have read other chapters such as Rules and Values Chapter 6 and Bad Behaviour Chapter 7. Children with really serious behaviour problems are very few indeed and the problems can usually be traced to a physical or emotional cause.

1. Make a list of the behaviours that you think are serious.

2. Ask your partner to make a list, are they the same?

3. Think back to when you think these problems first started, what was your child like then?

4. How does your child's behaviour compare to his or her peers?

5. Are your expectations reasonable for your child's age and abilities?

6. Read through the chapter. Do you recognise your family style as any I have discussed?

Serious Misbehaviour

All children "misbehave" at some time. This chapter describes children who have been so damaged and hurt by adults that their behaviours have become unacceptable and are seen as extreme.

For many years I have worked with children and young people who have come to me with labels such as "bad", "naughty" or "uncontrollable". Parents and teachers see them as wilfully difficult and disobedient. On the surface this may appear to be so, yet I have never worked with a young person so described who has not suffered considerably in some way.

Children, who exhibit behaviours that can be described as difficult, delinquent, violent, etc. have always been damaged, usually by those adults responsible for their care. Alice Miller (1991) is unequivocal when she says,

> *"so-called 'difficult', 'insufferable' children have been turned into such by adults."*

Children are never born bad. They are born into particular circumstances that help shape and influence their minds. Their personalities respond to environments and situations. It is these things that help to create a person. These children very frequently have parents who were themselves damaged as children. They repeat the pattern discussed in the introduction. No one is to blame for this situation. It is common to blame the parents, but when they are working from a faulty internal model that passes for good parenting (and is not conducive to having happy well adjusted children), then how far does one go back in time to lay blame? It is entirely unproductive to lay blame. However it is necessary to understand that until the damaging ways that are used to manage children, or the damage done because of a family pattern, is recognised then there is no possibility of change happening. I do recognise that parents are themselves very likely to be carrying damaged internal children of their own. No parent that I have met has deliberately wanted to damage their children. They may on occasions have been so angry that they have wanted to hurt them but, most parents that I have met have wanted to do their best for their children and have been grateful for some insight to their own behaviour and for some alternative strategies to use. The purpose of this chapter is to help parents who believe their children are seriously misbehaving to understand why, and think how their own behaviour contributes to that behaviour.

The reason I discuss them in this way is to help parents identify any actions of their own that might aggravate an already difficult situation and help to put it right. If there is any blame to be placed it is with a faulty internal model that gives rise to beliefs and practices that cause more problems than they remedy. The work of John Bradshaw (1991/93) is helpful for adults looking to heal their wounded inner child. I acknowledge that parents themselves are usually, doing their best, even when they know things are going wrong and say their children are out of control.

Some children, as already noted, are difficult for other reasons such as ADHD (Attention Deficit Hyperactivity Disorder). This chapter is not about children with those sorts of problems. It is intended to help parents who may be experiencing severe types of difficulties, to identify what their problems are and how they arise.

Children who have experienced a severe trauma or been deprived of the right sort of love have been spoiled. They are damaged emotionally and without that damage being acknowledged and understood, then nothing can be done to repair the problem. A common factor that often seems to be missing is unconditional love and acceptance. I am not suggesting that all parents of difficult children do not love their children. It is how they love them that is often so damaging; the absence of unconditional love is frequently a factor.

What usually happens is that adults are judgmental about the child and believe the fault to be entirely within the child. It is because many adults have within themselves their own hurt and damage from childhood and it is safer to blame the bad child (as probably happened to them) than to see the misbehaviour for what it is - pain. In order to do that it is necessary to recognise that some parents cause their children pain. The sort of pain that many parents inflict on their children in the guise of discipline is endorsed by society, for example through the media and politicians. Within society children seem to be seen as threatening and difficult to deal with. The younger generation with their new ideas and ways have, throughout history been threatening to an older generation . So, when thinking about discipline it appears easier and safer to continue with ineffective old beliefs than to try to stand back and really analyse and to look hard at what is happening. It is so often safer not to question, just to go ahead and punish the "perpetrator" rather that look for new ways to encourage self discipline.

What we so often need to do is to understand our inner child. To make that inner child less confused and afraid. By working on that aspect of ourselves and so improving our feeling of security and positive outlook we will begin to break the cycle of damage.

> *"... it is absolutely impossible for someone who has grown up in an environment of honesty, respect and affection ever to feel driven to torment a weaker person in such a way as to inflict lifelong damage" (Miller 1991:191-2).*

The reasons for misbehaviours

For many years I have noticed that children can use both active and passive strategies in their misbehaviours. By active strategies I mean violent behaviour, shouting, extremely violent temper tantrums, etc. Passive strategies would include 'accidents', 'forgetting' and deliberate incompetence. Elective mutism, where a child chooses to be silent is a good example of an extreme passive strategy. My observations have been confirmed by the work of Rudolf Dreikurs, (1970). He talked in terms of the 'goals of misbehaviours', defined as attention, power, revenge and inadequacy. Each 'goal' has its own driving force and means of expression. This seems a very good way of explaining misbehaviours that derive from serious malfunctions within the child's early experiences. (By early I mean experiences that happen while a child is still dependent on an adult for food, clothes and shelter - thus up to mid-teens.) I have used the four goals of misbehaviour as headings within this chapter.

Attention

All children need attention, which goes without saying. They should have received the loving, attentive gaze of their mothers from the moment they were born. They should have received a degree of quality or alone time (Gordon 1974) throughout their childhood. Because of their parents' inability, lack of time, etc., many children do not receive enough attention. They therefore become attention needing. As an experienced professional it is possible to spot a needy child almost the second one walks into the room. Eye contact is usually made immediately with such a child, and within a few moments some form of verbal, even physical contact, is made. I am often told that such-and-such a child is "attention seeking" - yes, it is usually true, and it is because they are attention needing. Confident, relaxed children whose self-image is good and self-esteem is high do not need to inappropriately seek attention. Strategies that attention needing children might use include:

Active:
Being demanding, uncooperative, excessively co-operative, always asking to help or do jobs. Not allowing you to have a conversation or time alone, 'needing' your presence.

Passive:
'Needing' help, becoming ill, always requiring coaxing or persuading. 'Forgetting'. Predicted and actual failure. 'Accidents'.

Power

These children have usually experienced parenting based on power or a total absence of it, (see Chapter 1 on parenting styles). Children who need to dominate are either repeating the role model they have experienced or they need to take control because no one else does. This can be very difficult to deal with because children who use power become more and more entrenched as they get older. They will develop a need to be in control for survival or because it is their perception of what it is to be an adult. When adults respond to them with adult power this has the effect of reinforcing what they already know - that to be powerful and in control is the only way to be.

I was helping a very unhappy little boy who came from an apparently caring, comfortable home. He had the latest computer equipment; there were two or three family holidays a year. Sitting talking with the parents I was struggling to find answers to the questions such as - why is this child presenting as so 'naughty'? What is driving that behaviour? What is the goal?

The parents had assured me that everything was fine between them. It was my second visit when I witnessed a confrontation between the parents and the child. I had asked to see Robert for a while. He was outside playing with friends. The mother went to the door and called "Robert, will you come in now". The emphasis on the now seemed to be to be unnecessarily impolite. The request was ignored. Her body language changed and so did the words, to "Get in here now". Robert's reply was inaudible. She came in and said to the father that he would have to do it. Robert's father repeated the demand in the same way and with the same effect. So he put on his shoes and within a minute or two a surly Robert stumbled and fell into the room as his father propelled him along. I wondered how this would be managed when Robert was the same height and weight as his father?

Active strategies:
Include bullying behaviour, tantrums, being manipulative, uncooperative and defiant, being contrary and always demanding things their way. Rude to adults and putting peers down.

Passive strategies:
Being 'lazy' or uncooperative, being manipulative, refusal through forgetting, accidents, ignoring parents, killer looks.

Revenge

These children will be deeply hurt. They are likely to have at least one parent who was similarly deeply hurt as a child. The parenting style they will be used to is most likely to be violent and based on power. The driving feeling is likely to be rage. The child whose behaviour is driven by a need for revenge will in all probability be the most damaged. Such a child will find it almost impossible to trust. Adults around such a child will find the behaviours outrageous. The child will probably be described as 'horrible', 'unlikeable', and so on.

Active strategies:
Unprovoked violence, violent retaliation, over-the-top responses, self-mutilation, rudeness, extreme verbal aggression, destruction of property.

Passive strategies:
Total non-compliance through ignoring requests or overtures, killer looks, illness, 'accidents'.

Inadequacy

This in itself is a passive form of misbehaviour. It is a form of withdrawal from the demands of the world. Often children who become inadequate set very high standards for themselves that are in the first instance too high, and then become demoralised when they fail to reach their goals. Alternatively they have had goals set way beyond their early reach and they have chosen to become incompetent as a result of being so demoralised. "80% of learning difficulties are related to stress. Remove the stress and you remove the difficulties" Stokes in Dryden and Vos (1993).

Active strategies:
'Accidents', refusal to co-operate.

Passive strategies:
Incompetence, illness.

What to do for children affected in this way.
I have briefly outlined a range of misbehaviours, their goals and some of the reasons for those goals. In the following pages I describe the sort of remedial actions that can be taken for each goal.

Attention:
These children often feel that they are unloved and unlovable. Because they have no firm foundation of feeling loved, they feel that they do not belong anywhere. I have noticed that children whose parents go through divorce often become attention needing even when previously they were confident and happy. This is because their foundations are threatened. The security of two parents and their home base is undermined. Therefore it is necessary to make attention needing children feel more confident about themselves. This is for both the passive and active strategist. All children need to develop a positive self-image with attainable goals that will lead to high self-esteem (see Chapter 3 on Self-Concept).

Children using active strategies
Be sure you give these children some personal time alone when you can do something that interests them. Set the time aside. Ask them how they would like to spend it. When they are seeking your attention in an inappropriate way tell them that in order to gain your notice they do not have to behave inappropriately. Make this demonstrably true. Ignore as much inappropriate behaviour as possible and reward - with your notice, attention, approval, etc. - the appropriate behaviour. Your attention will increase the chances of a behaviour being repeated. This is true for wanted and unwanted behaviour.

> *My family spent one Sunday afternoon with several other families. One little boy was very difficult: rude to his parents, competitive with the other children, and generally talked of as being very attention seeking.*

He would be on the swing saying "Dad, Dad, look at me, Dad". His father took no notice. Eventually he would call "John, John, look at me, John" whereupon his father would notice. He usually then said "Don't call me John, I'm your father, call me Dad". This was repeated several times during the afternoon. It was after he'd smacked the boy for calling him John and interrupting him that I could contain myself no longer. I pointed out that he only usually noticed the boy when he called him John or did something 'naughty'. He was training his son very carefully and subtly to do naughty, attention-seeking things to gain his notice. He claimed not to want his son to call him "John", but only responded when he did.

Later John's wife said that she had pointed this out to her husband but he took no notice. He only noticed him when he was naughty. He simply did not give the boy any time of the right quality that would feed a positive relationship and encourage the boy to have positive feelings about himself.

Passive Strategists
These children will need all the work on encouraging a positive self-image already mentioned. They will need positive, encouraging time. They are helped by instruction accompanied by a confident prediction, "I'm sure you are able…" "I know you can…" Whatever goal is set should, of course, be well within the child's ability. Children who have got themselves into a downward spiral may find it safer to fulfil a prediction of failure rather than success.

Power
Children who have experienced a parenting style based on power are likely to be angry and carry a sense of frustrated impotence. Children whose parents have set no boundaries or whose inconsistent parenting has led to a need in the child to take control, are also likely to be angry because they are having to fulfil two roles - that of caretaker (parents' job) and that of child. They do not automatically hold power, they will have seized it. In the outside world they will not be allowed to hold and wield so much power. All children in this situation are likely to experience anger, frustration and extreme confusion. They need clear information about boundaries. They need love and positive self-image work.

Children who are active strategists and parents who are power strategists
If you are a parent using these methods you need to stop controlling only by power. You will lose your child when they become physically and/or emotionally grown up, they will not be able to accept total domination. Your child will have already begun to repeat the pattern and in order for them to feel grown-up they will only feel they belong when they are dominating and in control. Cease hostilities at once, while you are still in control. Stop the power game. Stop being manipulative or whatever else you do. Explain (if your child is old enough to understand) what you have been doing. Explain that you will try to do it differently in future - and genuinely try. Recognise what power strategies you use, be aware of your language. Make sure you are not using controlling, demanding language.

Looking back to my example of Robert refusing to come in, then being forced to by his parents. They had become fixed in a relationship that relied on parents' power. Robert felt angry about the way he was treated and had reached the point where he would only do something when forced to. He was pushing the boundaries of their power the whole time.

He would have felt more inclined to be obliging to his parents if they had said something along the lines of "I know you are enjoying your game and I'm sorry to interrupt but Mrs Bliss is only here for a few minutes and we need you to come in for a while. You can carry on with your game later."

* It is informational and he is told he can go back to it later.
* That would acknowledge his irritation at leaving his game.
* On my next visit I did just that, to show how to get Robert's co-operation, and they thought I was a magician. Polite, empathic requests can have that effect on children.

Which would make you feel like responding: the above request, or "Get in here now"?

Stop modelling power and bullying methods. When children become uncooperative do not try to manipulate, force or coerce. Use humour, ask for their help (beware of manipulation), step down a notch and get alongside them. Remember to say please and thank you. Don't insist on total compliance. Negotiate, be prepared to give ground, be honest about your behaviour, and understanding of theirs.

Children who are passive strategists
Stop modelling power and bullying methods. Your child is quite possibly intimidated into passivity. Acknowledge effort, never name call. Understand about accidents. Use all the ideas recommended for children who are active strategists.

Parents who are too permissive
These parents will be exerting too little control, to the point where the child feels for its own safety that someone should. The child will be angry at having to take control and their use of power is very often to do with a misunderstanding of how to take control. They are also likely to be trying to force their parents into a position where they will take control and responsibility. These parents usually need outside help and support to feel strong and capable enough to take the reins. Not always though, and if you recognise your style as the "laissez faire" style in Chapter 1, then step back and examine what is going on. Think how you can be strong enough to take control and support your child. If the task seems too daunting, seek help.

Children who are active strategists
These children are likely to be viewed as rude, bullies, etc. People will wonder how parents put up with it. It is important to take control, to be assertive without being aggressive, to explain what you are doing and why you are doing it. You need to be reassuring

and consistent. You need to see things through and not to give up in the face of angry opposition, because it will be there for sure.

Passive strategists
They will be following your role model. It will be confusing when you start to change so explain what's going on and why you are behaving differently. Use all the ideas above.

Revenge

This is probably one of the most difficult motives to deal with. Children whose difficult behaviour is driven by a need to hurt, as they have been hurt are likely to be the most damaged. Perversely they will only feel they belong when they are damaging others, as they themselves have been hurt and damaged (see Miller 1987).

The parents of these children are likely to have inadvertently done the early damage and will probably need outside help to resolve the anger and pain that will be in their household. These parents will most likely be acting from a faulty internal model. The pain will be theirs as well as their child's.

The only way to heal a child so damaged is through love and trust. Developing a loving relationship that is full of implicit trust takes a very long time - probably years. It is important to remove punishments from the list of strategies. Such a hurt child will see these as retaliations. Adults dealing with these children need a great deal of support themselves, because only through love and understanding and by ignoring all the hurtful retaliative words and actions will progress be made. This is a difficult thing to do and requires exceptional patience and maturity on behalf of the adults that are in control.

Inadequacy
These children's self-image will be very poor. They will be completely disheartened by their apparent failure to achieve. Initially it is important to lower the standards expected. Encourage even the smallest achievement. Remind the child of what they can actually do. Compare current achievements with what they did before. Make it safe to achieve and move forward. Children whose "goal" is the protection of incompetence will be frightened by the thought of responsibility, achievement and successes. They will feel safer in failure because that will be the image that they hold of themselves.

Unconditional love is essential. Parents of these children are likely to have given conditional love. An empathic response to their negative feelings will also help, for example "I know you find this difficult" or "I can see the effort this requires for you".

Lots of patience is required to help repair the damage done. The child's response to that damage will in part reflect his or her personality and the belief system s/he holds. It will take a very long time to rebuild the child's ability to trust and to have the confidence to move forward to achieve successes, and feel comfortable with the resulting feelings. Below is the acronym P.R.E.P. this will be useful as a reminder of what will be needed for children who believe they are inadequate. All these strategies will take time and patience. It will not be easy.

> **P** ⇒ **Patience**
> **R** ⇒ **Reassurance**
> **E** ⇒ **Encouragement**
> **P** ⇒ **Praise**
>
> PREP will in time help eliminate feelings of incompetence. A child who feels so inadequate that s/he cannot cope with even the smallest challenges will need vast quantities of PREP in order to feel secure enough to try.

Summary

All children, from the moment they come into this world, have a right to unconditional acceptance and love. Very few receive it. This is because many parents carry within them a model of a parent who is unaccepting, hurtful (psychologically), critical and demanding. They also have an inner child who was on the receiving end of all that pain. In order to break these cycles of damage, we, the adults, must listen to ourselves. We are all the sum total of our experience and the way we respond to situations in our lives usually depends on prior learning. As parents we return to the internal model we learnt unconsciously as children. Much of that learning takes place in the early formative years and we can break the cycles of creating damaged, unhappy children by understanding how it happens.

In this chapter I have been discussing children who are likely to be very damaged and therefore show extremes of behaviour. But most of us carry some hurts from our childhood. For most people those hurts do not make them dysfunctional, but can influence their relationships throughout their lives. Unfortunately the damaged part of the self becomes forgotten, but the responses to it form part of a person's behavioural repertoire.

If only every parent truly understood themselves. If they could hear and feel the early pain they would be far less likely to repeat it. We need to understand ourselves before we can understand what we are doing to our children. Carl Rogers (1969) knew this when he said,

"I find I am more effective when I can listen acceptantly to myself, and can be myself."

Advice for Parents

Serious Misbehaviours

1. Your child has a right to unconditional love.

2. You may disapprove of the behaviour, never the child.

3. Always protect your child's self-concept.

4. Show respect. A child who has experienced respect is in a much better position to give respect.

5. Negotiate rules and decisions where possible once your child is old enough.

6. Give time for your child's interests.

7. Try to remember what it was like to be a small powerless child in a world where adults make all the rules.

8. Listen to your own inner child.

Parents' Questions

Chapter 11 - Bad Language

Ask yourself:

1. What constitutes bad language for you?

2. Are there times when you are either able to ignore or accept it?

3. How acceptable is it: on television, in cinema films or in the theatre?

4. Did your parents swear when you were a child?

5. If yes, in what context?

6. How did they react if you or any of your siblings swore?

7. In retrospect, did you approve of the response?

8. Have you any friends who swear?

9. How do you feel about their use of bad language?

10. What do you believe you and your partner should do about bad language?

Bad Language

All children hear bad language at school. It does not matter what school your child goes to, bad language knows no class barriers, your child will hear bad language and is likely to use swear words at some time with their own peer group. Often your child will have heard some bad language even before starting school.

Bad language is an emotive and subjective topic. Often, as a teacher, parents have complained to me about their children's language, though their own expletives have shown me where the children first heard such words. Some adults accept it amongst themselves but are thoroughly disapproving when they hear their children swear. If you swear, please do not be surprised. They will simply be imitating adult behaviour.

This is an area where things have undoubtedly changed in recent years. Very young children shock their parents by using some words without knowing what they mean. By the time children are seven they will have heard a considerable number of words that most parents did not hear at that age. They are unlikely to have any understanding of the concepts behind the vocabulary.

Some parents encourage bad language by finding it amusing to hear such a little tot using particular words. They laugh, and encourage repetition. This can be confusing for the child if at a later time they are told not to swear. If you hear words you do not wish your little one to use, the best policy is to ignore it wherever possible.

Many parents are upset and shocked by bad language amongst children. Occasionally my children have stopped me in my tracks with words I cannot believe they could have heard at say, seven years old. The apparent loss of innocence is not real because they have never understood the meaning of the words, and I never explain. Usually when children use swear words or 'dirty' words in front of you they are looking for guidance and boundaries.

I advise children not to use words they do not understand, and to make quite sure that other adults do not hear them repeating such words. I acknowledge that other children use swear words and that they may want to with their friends. It is not something I want to hear or can condone, and leave it at that. Once out of your hearing your child will make the decision for itself about whether to swear or not, regardless of what you say. You can forbid them to swear. In my experience children make up their own minds. It is much better to discuss the matter with them. Put forward your feelings and leave it up to them. They are then much more likely to make the decision you want.

As a teacher, if swearing was reported to me I always took the line "It's a good job I didn't hear it". This form of telling tales is a good one to get another child into trouble; it boils down to one child's word against another (or group of children). The reporting of bad language is not worth pursuing, you will very likely be in a no-win situation and you could get it wrong because you may have been set up.

It is best to ignore as much bad behaviour as you can, and swearing is one such example. Out of your hearing your child will make judgements about what is best for him or her in a given social situation. They will go through different phases and in adulthood will probably do pretty much as you do.

Banning your child from associating with children who swear can put them into a very difficult position. I have worked with children who are good children, they want to get things right and they want to do what their parents have said, but it is almost impossible for them to comply.

> *I can remember Susan, a neat, pretty child who had real difficulties relating to the children in her year seven tutorial group. The school was a good school that parents fought to get their children into. Her parents had told her to have nothing to do with children who swore, she was not to sit next to them, nor was she to play with them. To her distress there was no one in her new form who did not at some time swear. In a very tearful session I had with her she explained through her sobs that her mother said she "wasn't that sort of girl".*
>
> *The problem for Susan was that she wanted to obey her parents but, given the people in her tutorial, she was not able to. Susan would berate the other girls who laughed at her. She then became the butt of their jokes. Her mother's advice was to stand up for herself. She was not very clear what this meant, so she tried hitting them when they teased her. She eventually even resorted to using bad language herself in retaliation. The other girls saw her as a pest "its like having an annoying little sister who is always telling tales" said one girl.*
>
> *The problem for Susan was that she was in a value collision with her class and a no-win situation with her parents' advice. She had no personal problems with accepting her parents' attitudes and advice, but she was not able to implement their wishes and behave in the way they demanded. She was also not sufficiently socially skilled enough to do the balancing act that most children manage.*

As a parent you need to be aware of your own use of 'bad' language. Remember you always, as a grown-up, model grown-up behaviour. Children will model their behaviour on yours, they will copy you. When the majority of children use language amongst their own social groups that they know is not acceptable to adults, there is an unspoken rule that they keep it to themselves. They are able to switch into adult acceptable speech the moment an adult appears. There is no harm in this; it is what children have always done. As parents, our best and most helpful contribution is to play it down, ignore it, be clear about language that offends you, and make sure your children know when not to use it.

Advice for Parents

Bad Language

1. Set the boundaries.

2. Be clear about the fact if you disapprove.

3. Watch your own language.

4. Get children to think about the implications.

5. Ignore what you can.

6. Understand and acknowledge that your children will inevitably hear it.

7. Help them to decide how they are to deal with it.

8. Banning swearing when your children are out of sight can cause them more problems.

Parents' Questions

Chapter 12 - Spoiling

1. What is a spoilt child?

2. Were you spoilt as a child?

3. If yes, how?

4. Were your siblings spoilt as children?

5. If yes, in what way?

6. Was any child in your family spoilt at the expense of another?

7. Have you ever discussed this aspect of your upbringing with your siblings?

8. Is a little spoiling acceptable sometimes?

9. If you answered yes to Question 8, by whom and when is it acceptable?

10. If you answered no to Question 8, why?

11. Did you feel you sometimes missed out as a child - for example that you did not have as many new clothes as other children?

Spoiling

When I use the term spoil, I use it in the way we would describe an over-cooked meal, we would say it was ruined or spoilt. My definition of spoiling to do with children's behaviour means I believe a child is in an unhealthy relationship that is full of problems. Spoiling is not an occasional treat or lots of fuss and attention at special times, such as birthdays. Spoiling is when adults' behaviour and reactions to a child allows damage to occur to their relationship and to the child's healthy psychological development.

It is to do with the balance of power between a child and adults. It is definitely not being loved too much - that is impossible. Every child has the right to receive total, unconditional love. Spoiling a child is not true love. A spoilt child will wield power, be demanding, manipulative and attempt to coerce parents into meeting every whim or apparent desire. Unfortunately because such parents do not meet the real needs of their child, no one is happy.

All children need to feel secure, they need boundaries. Therefore a child who is allowed to manipulate and be too powerful will have a sense of undue omnipotence it cannot understand. It will not know where the boundaries are, this will lead to anger, frustration and fear. After all, if parents offer no containment and therefore security, who will? Spoilt children are insecure, unhappy children.

Children who become spoilt are often greedy, lonely, dissatisfied and unhappy. They remain egocentric and so absorbed in their own needs that they are unable to understand that other people have needs. They gain very little satisfaction or pleasure from possessions because they already have so much and they are likely to be planning what they want next. Children who are spoilt are likely to be unpopular with others because they moan and complain. They are unable to share and are bad losers in games. Being used to bullying their parents they are likely to use the same strategies with others outside the house.

Truly spoilt children often feel unlovable because they have not had very basic bonding needs met at the beginning of their lives. For other children the spoiling may have started with an illness. The loving parents, in their distress and concern, may have quickly established a pattern of allowing demanding, rude behaviour that shifted the balance within their relationship. It can be so easily done, and once the illness is over, the spoiling continues.

Peer Pressure

There is considerable pressure on some children these days to acquire certain things such as computers, bicycles and brand name clothes. If you have included a certain healthy scepticism for advertisements and those sorts of pressures in your life at home, then this is less likely to be a problem to deal with than if you have not.

The mantra of "everyone else does/has" that can go up at regular intervals will increase if you respond to it. Parents who make an early stand with those complaints give themselves a much stronger position later on when requests are likely to come more frequently and be more expensive. When you are told "everyone else has ..." believe me, it is very unlikely. The reality will be that a small group may have a currently fashionable item of clothing or be going to see the latest film, but certainly not everyone. You have to be able to work within your cash limits. The cash available is for all the family. It is no good to anyone if you become a nervous wreck because you have over-bought for your children and you are not able to meet the repayments. Honesty, without over burdening your children, is the best policy. It will help them understand your need to balance a budget and the fact that you have lots of calls on your money.

When does spoiling start? Many people would say it begins with a crying baby. As crying is the only way for a baby to alert those taking care of it that there is a need for food or comfort, or a problem such as illness, a crying baby should not be ignored. If a baby has its needs met at an early stage then it will be less attention-needing later on. Indeed, ignoring the needs of a baby could lead to an insecure child with other problems. A child will learn that its needs are important within the context of family life.

Reasons for spoiling

There are many reasons why children become spoilt, such as:

* grandparents giving what they could not afford to give their own children
* overcompensation by an adult for a gap in their own lives
* illness
* lazy parenting
* misguided parenting
* thoughtless parenting, such as when parents are too busy
* separation, such as divorce or death
* peer pressure, keeping up with the "Joneses".

Some parents live with the pain of their own unhappy childhood. They may fear they will lose the love of their child if they say no. However, loving discipline as described in this book is good. Saying no is imperative sometimes. Children need and value a consistent structure.

Illness
The need for discipline still applies when a child is ill, long term illness is not helped by allowing a child to "rule the roost". A small gift such as a comic is fine, but basic everyday rules of common courtesy still apply. We can all feel irritable when we are ill but that does

not excuse a bad tempered or ill mannered demanding and it is still possible to manage a "thank you" to whoever has been fetching and carrying for the patient. I am not suggesting a major confrontation with a sick child if that happens - a gentle reminder is all that is necessary. Illness, especially if it is prolonged, can mean that the balance of power shifts, and the child is allowed to become too powerful and demanding in a way that is unhealthy and likely to be frightening for the child. It is important that parental consistency remains the same at a time such as illness, just as it is important to be reasonably consistent at other times, (see Chapters 6 and 7).

Loss

When children suffer a loss it is at that time that familiarity and consistency can become all important. The desire to compensate with material gifts is easily understood, but unnecessary and possibly damaging.

For divorced parents too much inappropriate giving is obviously symptomatic of deeper, unresolved problems. While it is usually the mother who has the bulk of day-to-day responsibility and the father has access rights at the weekend, this is not always the case. Many divorced parents who are the primary caretakers complain about the goodies and treats their children receive at weekends. Access to children should be about quality of time rather than a quantity of things. Absent parents are likely to experience a range of emotions such as guilt, sadness and loneliness away from their familiar family, even if the break has also brought relief from tensions and arguments between partners. The absent parent may feel a need to make amends for the absence. That will be best achieved by giving attention and time rather than things. Time should be spent reading together, playing games, walking, cooking, or whatever else the child considers is fun to do.

Grandparents

The problem of grandparents giving to children can be difficult. All children receive gifts from their grandparents but it has to be pitched at a level to suit the family. If the grandparents' giving causes problems then it has to be dealt with kindly but firmly by the parents. Some grandparents may overcompensate because when their children were young they were unable to give. They may be in competition with the main wage earner in the family, or using the giving for other unhealthy purposes. They may be doing all these things consciously or unconsciously. If their giving is in some way spoiling the relationship then it is unhealthy and needs to be tackled. Some grandparents make the mistake of allowing grandchildren to equate their love with the giving of material things, and children are disappointed if the things are not forthcoming. The grandparents have spoilt the relationship quite unconsciously. If the grandparents were in competition with the parents then that too would be unhealthy and unnerving for the child. In all cases the parents need to take control and establish rules and boundaries.

Sharing

Some children share their toys, sweets, etc. more readily than others. In part it depends on their personality. It can also depend on how you help them manage the situation in the early days.

Let's imagine the scenario of you being at a friend's home where there is a child the same age as your child. It can be very difficult for you both if the child whose home it is refuses to share any of the toys, and even more so if the parent ignores the problem. You will probably be trying to hold a conversation with your own unhappy child complaining about mistreatment. You will be trying to listen to your friend and your child while thinking "How do I deal with this?"

Children can understand the value of sharing from a relatively early age. When discussing the value of sharing it is possible to develop embryonic feelings of empathy for one's fellow human beings. For example, a reminder of how upset she felt on an occasion when another child would not share with her will enable your child to gain a little insight into how another child might feel.

I found that it saved problems if I discussed with my little ones what toys they did not want to share, before friends arrived. It is perfectly understandable that some things may be too new or too special to share. Those special things went away out of sight for the duration of the visit. By the age of four they were able to make decisions for themselves about sharing, without my help. Some children were allowed access to all their special toys while others were not. The discussions about sharing which we had prior to visits also prepared the ground. They knew what to expect and very early on became skilled hosts, treating visitors with special care.

In observing children who find sharing their toys difficult, I notice it appears that they are often also unprepared for sharing their parents with visitors. They resent the intrusion into their home space, then having to share their toys is the last straw. Preparing the ground with children enables them to anticipate situations and helps them to anticipate what will be likely to happen in particular social situations. It needs to be done on a regular basis at first. All learning is a slow process requiring repetition and practice, social skills are no exception. Being a good host requires social skills of a high order. Learning to share at home is a part of that learning. It will also have beneficial effects in other areas of life such as school.

An Only Child

Having just one, precious child can present unique problems to parents. It is easy to spend an unhealthy amount of time and resources on an adored only child. Only children can become such a focus of parents that it prevents natural healthy psychological growth within the family. An only child does not necessarily mean a spoilt child. I have very fond memories of a childhood friend of mine who was an only child. She was very generous but balanced in her dealings with her peers.

Only children who receive an unhealthy amount of parental attention will be ill at ease in wider society. It will be natural for them to have more attention than a child who is one of three or four. But parents have needs of their own. They should have interests beyond their child. A child given an unhealthy amount of attention is burdened by those parents. The child's own psychological development is likely to become stunted or twisted by the weight of such a focus. So parents remember it is good for you to have time to yourself, time with your friends, and time away from your child. Equally your child will need time away from you, time with his/her own friends, and time of their own to just be themselves.

All the discussion above applies to families with just one child. Where there is only one child it is necessary to expose that child to his/her peers. An only child needs lots of opportunities to play with children of the same and different ages. One area they often find difficulty with is coping with younger children. If only children are used to peers where the context is one of relative equality, or of older children who make allowances for them, they never have to experience the trials and tribulations that frustrating younger children can mean. Coping with irritations and frustrations is a necessary part of the learning process. It may be an area of social learning that only children miss out on.

Advice for Parents

Spoiling

1. Do not just give in - that is lazy parenting. A child will come to learn that if they keep on then you will eventually give in.

2. Be consistent about your ground rules. You should have thought them through. If your child is constantly challenging them, make sure they are fair and reasonable.

3. When you say no - mean it. Stick to your no, regardless of the tantrums, they will become shorter and less frequent as time passes.

4. Encourage choice. Give your child times when they can choose and it does not really matter to anyone except them, e.g.. what cereal to eat for breakfast, or what clothes to wear at the weekend.

5. Question the request - not every time, but when it is appropriate. Do it in a gentle, friendly, open way, e.g. "So you feel you need new trainers? How much did you say they were? And what did you say was wrong with the old trainers?" Encourage your child to think about the request. If necessary, state the facts about the financial position. Encourage thoughts about the needs of other members of the family, including yourself.

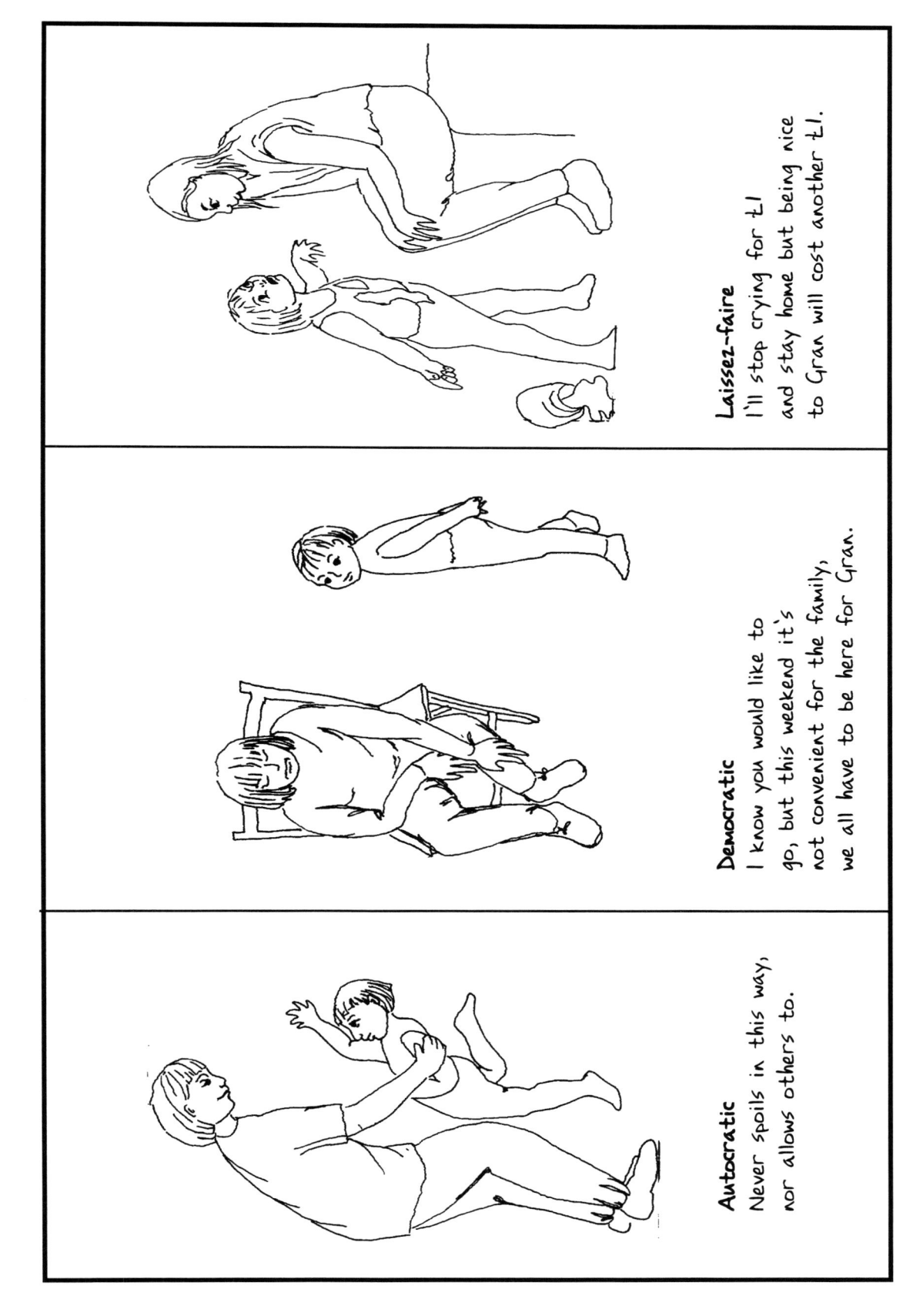

Autocratic
Never spoils in this way, nor allows others to.

Democratic
I know you would like to go, but this weekend it's not convenient for the family, we all have to be here for Gran.

Laissez-faire
I'll stop crying for £1 and stay home but being nice to Gran will cost another £1.

Parents' Questions

Chapter 13 - Encouraging Independence

1. What does this phrase mean to you?

2. How do you encourage it in your child?

3. What decisions do you allow?

4. How did your parents encourage your independence?

5. What life skills do you believe you possessed when you left home?

6. Did you have to fight for your independence?

7. Do you believe that by encouraging independence you will encourage your child to go away from you?

8. In how many areas can you allow your child the freedom to practice making choices?

9. Can you increase those opportunities?

Encouraging Independence

Most parents want confident, self-reliant, responsible children who are able to make the right choices for themselves in the adult world. Sadly many parents start life with their children using the authoritarian style of management. The majority then go on to abandon that style in favour of doing nothing, because parents lack alternatives and children become, as one mum said to me, "too old and too stroppy" resulting in permissiveness in order to save their relationship with their child. Children with authoritarian or permissive parents will not be the best equipped to deal with life. It is these parents who experience some of the most tempestuous of teenage years.

Children of authoritarian parents will be used to being controlled and directed by their parents. They will have had little opportunity to make decisions for themselves. They will not be used to taking responsibility or making choices because their parents would have done it all for them. Often children from authoritarian homes are the most rebellious in the teenage years. They are not used to taking decisions and handling responsibility and will not do it well at first. They may also have a backlog of anger and frustration to clear. The majority of these young people go through a turbulent maturing process relatively unscathed, but not all (see Chapter 1).

Permissive parents who have given in to their children's demands, have allowed too many, too flexible, or undefined boundaries, may not necessarily have children who are totally out of control. Society can have a controlling influence on, for example, the prevention of criminal behaviour in youngsters. However they are likely to have children who in the context of home expect to have demands met, are uncooperative, exacting and very self-centred. Their understanding of their responsibilities will be distorted, they will be used to making egocentric decisions without reference to the needs or wishes of others. The teen years are again likely to be turbulent. They are likely to be very selfish adults with poor quality peer relationships. Some will look back in horror at their behaviour. There may well be a period of anger and/or bewilderment at their parents' levels of tolerance. Most will survive the maturing years, with their relationship with their parents just about intact.

The group who are likely to carry responsibility with the greatest of ease and relish independence as young adults, are those whose parents have largely favoured the democratic approach. They will be used to making choices for themselves and taking decisions with reference to others. They will have experienced their opinions being sought and valued. They will be likely to be assertive without being aggressive. They will be the best equipped of the three groups to make good quality decisions for themselves.

It is important not to force independence before your child is ready. Most children will set a pace that you will be happy to follow. Some children need encouragement in some areas.

They are all very different. Some children will be very content to remain at home and see few other children, some children on the other hand are desperate for peer group company. All groups will need to be exposed to peers for different reasons.

Making Choices

It is possible to start at a very young age encouraging children to make simple guided choices for themselves. They will look to you as a role model. If they see you approving of certain things, they will copy you. Some parents make the mistake of imposing certain values and attitudes at too early an age, with the result that from curiosity or perversity, the child chooses the opposite position.

> *A friend of mine insisted that her pre-school age son should never have a gun. She and her husband were pacifists, and took the view that their children would adopt that attitude as well. In all other respects they seemed a mixture of democratic/permissive parents, except on this one issue, where they were dogmatically authoritarian. Ben became obsessed with the thought of having a gun to play with. Every time he came to our house he sought out the gun. At his house he fashioned guns out of Lego and bits of wood. Because Ben was denied a gun, to own one became more and more important to him. His mother spent hours explaining how she hated guns and her belief in non-violence. It all went over his four year old head. She would have been more successful if she had said to him that although she did not approve, if a gun was his greatest wish, he could have one.*

My husband and I took the view that when our children were very little they would have guns if, say, someone bought one for them, or they particularly wanted one. It seemed each time one of our children became four years old they expressed an interest and we occasionally had several guns around the house for short periods. We did not make an issue out of it, we did not ourselves play guns with them. Within a very short space of time the gun phase passed. We do not have gun or violence obsessed youngsters, quite the opposite in fact. It seems to me that one of the attractions for children of playing with guns is the adults' reaction. Most are willing to play along and stand with their hands in the air or fall down "dead". This is great fun, and gives the child a feeling of power, and is nothing whatever to do with the reality of guns. The best way forward, I believe, is to allow these "toys" but refuse to join in. Just say that it is not a game you like to play. The interest will die away naturally for something more rewarding to do with you.

Play is a preparation for life. It is a greater preparation in many ways than school. The most important part of a school day to the majority of children is the time they can spend in free association with their friends - play time. In pre-school play groups I hear mothers shaping their children's identities with phrases such as "little girls/boys do ...", or "little boys/girls don't ...", or "you're a little girl/boy, you should ...". While tiny tots are associating with peers, mothers and fathers so often define their children by their sex, then tell them what they should or should not say or do. In so doing they restrict their choices and limit their access to certain activities, for example "little boys don't dress up like that" or "little girls wear pretty clothes, you're a little girl, you put on the hat", "no David, you can't wear the beads, boys don't wear beads", or "let the boys have the trucks, boys like to play with cars".

These are snatches of conversations I have recorded at various times. I used to feel saddened and frustrated by this early sexual stereotyping but it happens all the time. It encourages children to reject particular activities on the basis of their gender and channels them into particular circumscribed occupations befitting a boy or a girl, thus denying real choice.

As I have already said, words are powerful tools. The words you use to your child will help to shape the psyche, self-concept and behaviour for the rest of his or her life.

Choose your words with care, remember they are seeds planted into your child's memory bank. Once said, they will remain on deposit for good or ill.

Young children need help and encouragement to choose. It is best to start with things you do not really mind about. If you have a particular outcome in mind for an activity or course of action, then you will be unlikely to offer a genuine choice or your method of giving that choice may not be as open as it should. The sorts of activities children can make choices about are, for example, whether to have a game or a story just before bed or watch TV... right up to bed time. They can choose what clothes to wear outside school time, who to play with, what to spend their pocket money on. Give them some real choice in where the family goes for the day on outings. For them to have real practice at making choices and coping with the results and responsibilities of those decisions, then the choice must be genuinely theirs to make, without prejudice or coercion from you, otherwise it is all a pretence.

One of the traps I fell into with my first child was offering her choices before she was really ready for them. They were simple choices such as which jumper would she like or which flavour ice cream. Children become ready to make choices at different ages. As a sensitive parent you will discover when that time has come. You will make the choices safe and simple, and at the right level for your child. Gradually the decision making will be extended and built upon. As with all things in life, we need practice in order to become competent, and independence is one of them.

Later on they can make choices about joining clubs, whether to have an extra swimming lesson or take up dancing. Within the context of how you believe you should shape your child's life, it is best to give them as much choice as possible. I have seen little girls pressured into dancing and taking the exams, only to thankfully abandon it as soon as they feel strong enough to resist their parents. Likewise I have witnessed little boys' entire leisure time dominated by rugby. At first they believe that they are enjoying themselves, but again, abandon it as soon as they are able to resist adult pressure.

> *One perceptive boy I worked with hated rugby but continued to go. His father was the team coach and the two were clearly in a vicious circle. The son Michael understood this. When I asked him why he continued to go, he said it was for his father. He explained that his father used to love to play but no longer could, because of injury, however he had a great deal of pleasure in watching a naturally gifted son. He also believed it was his only point of contact with his father. Michael did not value much that his father stood for, he felt bullied by him at home, and desperately wanted to leave, but he loved his father and valued his father's love. He wanted to leave on good terms and hoped to be able to drift away from rugby without causing a rift. He was planning on looking at universities where rugby was not played.*

Michael had made a very mature choice. He had chosen to continue with rugby to please his father, and to continue with something in which his father was interested in order to spend time with him. He believed his father had done the best he knew how. Michael's mother had died when he was fourteen and he had come to me because he was experiencing problems at school. The problems were at home but, as so often happens, they surface at school. It appeared that Michael's mother had been a democratic parent who mediated with his father. His father had spent long periods away from home so Michael had been largely brought up by his mother. It appeared that it was her influence that had given him the strategies he used to cope with his father.

> *Recently I was chatting to a mother while waiting for my son to finish his swimming lesson. She asked why my daughter did not attend swimming classes, I said because she had decided not to this term. She looked at me with a very puzzled "Oh?" then said "You give her a choice?" To which I replied that my children always had a choice about their activities outside school. She said it simply would not occur to her to ask her children, they swam and danced because she organised it. She said she thought learning to swim was particularly important. I explained that my daughter swam quite well for a six year old, and had some distance badges, and that was enough to satisfy her. This mother made it clear that she thought I was too permissive for her tastes and that children should do as many out of school activities to ensure as broad an education as possible.*

She could be right, maybe her children will thank her. Perhaps my children will grow up to say I should have pushed them in this direction or that. We all have to do what our experience, understanding and beliefs dictate is best. One of the gifts we can give to our children is to encourage in them an ability to organise a satisfying life for themselves through making good quality choices.

Whether circumstances actually allow them to achieve all they wish for is another matter, but we can start by offering them choices, then through genuinely informative discussion (not persuasion, or directing them one way or the other) help them to make decisions about their lives that will be right for them, rather than how we wish them to be. Thus when they reach the teenage years of growing independence they will know how to choose, and do it well.

Encouraging Independence

Making choices and taking decisions is part of encouraging independence. Another aspect is allowing your children to do things for themselves and by themselves. Early on it can be difficult because, quite frankly, it is easier to put on socks, button blouses and lace shoes yourself. The majority of children enjoy becoming independent and learning how to handle potentially difficult situations.

As soon as our children could walk and showed interest in the stairs, we taught them how to negotiate the stairs. We never had one of our children fall down. We did have stair gates, but that was at the top to prevent accidental falling down. I have know children climb over stair gates to get up or down - a very dangerous thing to do.

We have nearly always lived near busy roads with heavy traffic. We taught the children to cross the road safely as soon as we felt they could cope which was usually as young as 4. They have all shown great caution with traffic. Sometimes our children had their friends to stay, who were not allowed to cross the road. Often these children had not been given the opportunity to develop any road sense, and their lack of independence in this area was always a great worry to me.

The rule that seems to work best is, if you want your child to develop a skill in any area, then you have to let them practise. It is best if you show them in a calm and patient manner, allowing them to practise the skill while you watch. You will then know your child's level of competence, and be able to leave them to it. Obviously some things you will want to supervise for some time.

If children are competent at things it gives them a certain status with their peers.

> *One little boy I remember was not academically very bright, but the one thing he could do when he was six was tie shoe laces. He loved to be in demand at the end of PE lessons. Children who are totally incompetent and unable to do things for themselves are looked down upon by their peers. A nine year old came into my class in the middle of the*

school year. We went swimming and I told the children to get ready. He stood and did nothing, but when I mentioned him by name he dropped his towel and put his arms in the air. I asked him what he was doing and he said "Getting ready, come on I'm ready" – he had never dressed himself before! He stood bewildered when we came out of the pool, not knowing where to start. He needed training like a baby and was not at all impressed at the imposition of having to do things for himself! One of the reasons he had come to me was because he was still too dependent on his mother. His parents were extremely permissive and protective. He bullied and made demands on them. They were helpless and needed professional help to help themselves in the face of their young tyrant's onslaughts.

Another child with a more independent personality would have objected to being treated in such a way, but this one did not.

Some parents deny their children independence because they fear losing them. The latter group of parents misunderstand the nature of emotional attachment between parents and children. The more you prepare your child for coping with life and help them to develop as an independent person, the more likely you are to have a good quality relationship with them when they grow up. Children who are encouraged to be independent will be more confident. They will have greater self-awareness and a more positive self-image. Without any encouragement children compare and contrast themselves with one another. If they have a greater number of skills than others then they will feel more competent. Children who are unnecessarily denied experiences and opportunities can be, in some ways, deprived.

Allowing and encouraging independence is not the same as neglect or ignoring your child. I am talking about allowing children to make choices at a level that is appropriate for them and experiencing independence with your full knowledge, not your neglect. A child who feels trusted and encouraged by his or her parents is much more likely to feel positive towards them, and to feel competent and happy at home. That positive self-image and belief in themselves will be carried into the wider world. A child encouraged towards the fullest independence possible will be much more ready and able to deal with life in school and beyond than a dependent child unable to cope or fend for itself.

Advice for Parents

Encouraging Independence

1. Allow your child to start making simple choices about food and clothes as early as possible.

2. Discuss the outcomes of these choices.

3. Remind them of past successes.

4. Be confident that good choices will be made.

5. Teach your child how to do things for him/herself as soon as possible, e.g. cross the road, use the microwave, and so on.

Parents' Questions

Chapter 14 - Praise and Rewards

1. What do these two words mean to you?

2. Were you conscious of being praised and/or rewarded by your parents?

3. If yes, how did you feel?

4. If no, how did you feel about that then and what do you feel about that now?

5. What are your beliefs about praise and rewards now?

6. When should praise be used?

7. When should rewards be used?

8. Do your ideas match your partner's?

Praise and Rewards

It is important that we support and encourage our children. We know that if they find something rewarding they are likely to repeat it. Unfortunately some parents turn a good thing into a bad thing. Praise and reward is a valuable commodity and should be used with care and caution. If praise and rewards are used to control children you will soon undermine their value. If you use the promise of them as a bribe or the removal of them as a threat then you will quickly find you have run out of currency or devalued it, so that the cost of keeping up with inflation is too high.

Many parents undermine the positive value from two common motives, one is to encourage children along a chosen path or course of action, the other is to prevent children from taking a chosen path or course of action. Either way praise and rewards are used as agents of control. This can lead to children feeling entrapped, resentful, unhappy and ultimately doing the exact opposite to what the parents intended.

Another motive for praising children that always has the opposite effect is to cheer them up. I heard an example of this recently at a swimming gala.

> *A child had been placed fourth and was obviously disappointed by her performance. Her mother gushed "Katie you were wonderful you did so well. I am so proud of you." She could see the look on her daughters face, she continued "Coming fourth doesn't matter you were really good I am so pleased with you." The girl flounced off to get dressed. Her need at the time was for her mother to listen and acknowledge her disappointment, not to dismiss it out of hand!*

The mother's need was clearly to cheer up her child and preserve her self-esteem. That would have been achieved if she had acknowledged her disappointment and her effort and said what pleasure it gave her just to see her competing. Perhaps a more appropriate comment might have been. *"I was thrilled to see you in that competition. How do you feel you did?"* The girl could then express some disappointment. Her mother could have empathised with her disappointment with words that reflected what her daughter had said. The conversation might have continued like this,
"I didn't win, I'm fed up I tried really hard to come first."
"It's disappointing when we don't win when we've tried our hardest."
A hug might also have helped but words that deny true feelings can make things worse.

Power

The person who gives rewards and praise is in a very powerful position. Unjustified praise can be confusing. I can remember making that mistake with one of my daughter's paintings. It was some time later that she told me when I inappropriately praised her pictures it had the effect of making her feel fobbed off and patronised. A salutary thought, that made me think very carefully in future. Praise is not always necessary in those circumstances but interest is. Better responses to a child waving a picture are:

* "Tell me about it" or
* "That looks interesting" or
* "Those colours make me feel ..."

The use of rewards as bribes is very much a power issue. It also sometimes sets children and their parents up to fail. I am always unhappy to hear that parents have offered huge rewards for satisfactory school reports. This is potentially so damaging and undermining to future school work, and to the parent-child relationships.

At best, school reports are a subjective guide to your child's behaviour. Teachers are human beings, they are under a great deal of stress and pressure. In a primary school teachers are likely to have between thirty and forty children to deal with. In a secondary school it could be between three and five hundred children they see each week. Teachers miss things, they make subjective judgements. They get things right, they get things wrong. Huge rewards should not rest on reports when the child has no real control over the outcome.

Research has shown that by rewarding children to do what they would do anyway, it is possible to undermine their motivation. For example, most children will paint pictures because it is pleasurable to do so. When a group of four year old children were rewarded for painting, they stopped wanting to paint when the rewards were taken away. (Wright 1990). If things are going well at school you will receive a good report. If they are going badly you can offer the moon and you will not receive a good report.

Rewards are very much a double-edged sword. Treat them with the same respect and care. If you want to give your child a treat just for the sake of having a treat, say so. Avoid making it a payment otherwise she will be looking for more payments and be put off working for the pleasure of seeing a piece of work well done!

Unhelpful Praise

Praise is so often judgmental such as "good boy/girl" or "well done", when all the child is looking for is interest, not judgement. Praise can also be embarrassing.

> *One year my daughter won the child of the year shield at school, the reward for being an all-round nice person, well mannered, good-natured, considerate, helpful. As parents we were naturally proud that it went to her, and we showed everyone who came into the house. Sometimes she found it too embarrassing to cope with. We always warned her it was coming so that she could go away and hide until the adulation had died away.*

It is also not comfortable if the child does not agree with the adults' assessment.
> *At a social gathering a friend announced that her daughter Sarah was going to cut her hair. The adults around looked aghast at Sarah - Sarah with waist length angel's hair the colour and texture that no bleach bottle could emulate. Sarah's face went bright red and she stubbornly stood her ground in the face of considerable opposition. Maybe her*

mother was going to have to let her do this thing to herself. Certainly Sarah was fed up with hair that everyone admired. At fourteen some children need to exert their growing independence from their parents. Hair will grow again if necessary, and saying it is beautiful when it doesn't feel that way to the child will not make her change her perception of it.

Encouragement

The best form of praise is the language of encouragement. This is a way of speaking that is informational to your child, you explain precisely what you are pleased about without being judgmental. You speak only of their achievements and do not compare their achievements with what you achieved at that age or what siblings have managed. Some examples are:

Appreciation of effort
* *"Thank you for doing the washing up/tidying your room"*
* *"Its really helpful when you ..."*
* *"I appreciate ..."*

Giving trust in your child's ability
* *"I am confident you can ..."*
* *"I do believe you can do it"*
* *"I trust you to ..."*

Acknowledging effort
* *"That has obviously meant a lot of work"*
* *"If we look back at what you have achieved recently ..."*

Make your statement and leave it at that. Many people go on to detract from what they have said. An example is: "Thank you for tidying your room. Now why can't you do it all the time and save me nagging?" The first sentence was fine. When you notice effort, show a genuine interest, it will reinforce your relationship, and is likely to increase motivation next time. They will know and be shown that you care enough to take an interest. It will help self-esteem. It will make them want to repeat the behaviour.

The language of encouragement is used by the democratic parent.
* It is not judgmental, but rewarding and constructive.
* It states your position, your feelings, and does not then try to direct or control your child's behaviour in any way.
* It compares current status and progress with what has been achieved in the past.
* It tells them exactly why you are pleased and acknowledges the child's own effort.

This form of praise helps the cognitive (thinking) processes by encouraging internalisation and understanding of what they should be doing, why they should be doing it, and how to proceed in the future.

Advice for Parents

Praise And Reward

1. Give lots of thanks and praise to encourage the behaviours you want to see (it must be natural).

2. Be informational when you praise.

3. Compare their own past achievements with current achievements.

4. Never unfavourably compare them to anyone else.

5. Acknowledge and appreciate the effort they put into a task.

6. Your attention and time are the best rewards.

Parents' Questions

Chapter 15 - Listening

1. Do you consider yourself a good listener?

2. Would your parents have described themselves as good listeners?

3. Would you have agreed with them on their answer? Why?

4. Do you know someone who is an exceptional listener? What makes them good?

5. Do you know someone who never listens? What is it that they do?

6. When did you last really listen to your child, without interruption?

Listening

This is one of the most important chapters of this book. How may times do our children say, "You never listen?" Good quality listening is essential to a democratic parent. My training as a counsellor has taught me about listening. It is something I am told I am very good at in my professional life, but my children frequently complain that I do not listen to them. I lead a very busy life and unless I am careful I can make the mistake of trying to listen while I am cooking, have the radio on, or am doing something else. I have learned to say "I cannot give you my full attention right now, can it wait until later?" Usually it can - occasionally I have to stop to give them my full attention.

When I started my training I discovered that I was not a very good listener. Most people in normal social intercourse are not very good listeners. We assume that what normally takes place is we talk - someone listens. However what usually happens while listening is supposed to take place is:

Someone talks
> then we listen - we evaluate - we plan what we will say - we daydream - we rehearse what we will say - then jump in as soon as the talker stops!

What we jump in to say is not always helpful.

Several writers who give advice on listening skills agree that there are ways of responding that effectively stop further discussion. They are called roadblocks because they block communication. The roadblocks may be temporary or permanent. They are listed below, arranged in the categories Robert Bolton uses in his book "People Skills".

Judging by —
- Criticising
- Name calling
- Judging by Diagnosing
- Praising

Sending solutions by —
- Ordering
- Threatening
- Sending solutions by Moralising
- Questioning
- Advising

Avoiding issues by —
- Diverting
- Avoiding issues and concerns by "Logical" argument
- Reassuring

Judging

1. Criticising and blaming with you as the judge, e.g. "You're always ..." or "You want to ..."

2. Calling your child names or ridiculing, e.g. "You're a baby/wimp/silly" etc.

3. Interpreting, playing amateur psychologist, e.g. "You didn't manage that because you feel ...", "I know what you're like, its because ..."

4. Praising - evaluating as good even when the child knows it is not true.

Sending solutions

5. Directing, ordering, with you in control, e.g.. "In my house you ..."

6. Threatening or issuing warnings, e.g.. "If you don't ... I'll ..." or "You'd better do ... or else ..."

7. Moralising or preaching, e.g.. "You don't know how lucky you are", "Schooldays are the happiest days of your life"

8. Questions that are too probing and amount to interrogation, e.g. "How do you imagine you'll ...", and "Why on earth did you ..." They also divert the talker's train of thought away from what they really want to say.

9. Advising, offering ready made solutions that may only suit you, e.g.. "If I were you I'd ..." or "Why don't you ..."

Avoiding the other's concerns

10. Diverting - this is commonly done quite harmlessly with infants, but diverting means you withdraw from the problem and do not deal with it, e.g.. "Oh let's change the subject and talk about something nicer.". Questions can also be diverting and say more about the questioner's train of thought than the person supposed to be talking.

11. Logical arguments are often a lecture that is listened to politely then mentally dumped, e.g.. "Let's take a look at what is really happening here, if you hadn't spent your time in front of the TV this evening you'd have finished your homework".

12. Reassuring inappropriately. It is sometimes painful for us to witness others' pain. It is our need we are usually attending to when we reassure inappropriately, e.g.. "I'm sure it will be OK".

All the above responses are what can happen when a parent responds without really listening. They are responses that come from assumptions and expectations that will have nothing to do with the child's position. It can be very uncomfortable for a parent when a child is in distress. It may appear easier to divert and say "don't cry" than to deal with the problem. Often parents just do not have answers to problems or cannot deal with them. It can be simpler to prevent further communication by sending a roadblock. However, I assume that by reading this book you are trying to improve your skills and gain some new ideas for handling difficult situations. All of the books listed in the bibliography by Mazlish and Faber (1974) are quite brilliant in the way they illustrate how to listen and talk to our children.

> *One of the children I mentioned earlier was being stuck in grief for the loss of her grandmother. Her mother found her daughter's tears too painful to bear so she refused to allow any mention of her grandmother. The girl had been used to seeing this relative every day until she was seven. They had a loving and close relationship. Her mother blocked her daughter's ability to grieve. It was only when she allowed her to cry - and cried with her - that she began to recover. Now she has a photo of her grandmother beside her bed and they visit the grave less frequently. The girl's unexplained anger has gone.*

Listening is a difficult skill to learn from the printed page. Below are a few ideas to help. If you feel you are a poor listener and would really like to improve then look for a course on listening skills. Good courses offering an introduction to counselling will always contain work on listening.

Listening is not a passive skill. It requires a great deal of effort, attention and understanding. One powerful exercise I do with groups of adults is to put them into pairs and give each one of the pair a different instruction. The first person is instructed to think of something nice to tell the other about, such as a meal they enjoyed in a restaurant or an enjoyable day. The other person is told to look as though they are listening for the first 30 seconds, then lose eye contact, fiddle with clothes, effectively cease to show that listening is taking place. Most people dry up and are not able to continue talking, the person who has been instructed to stop making eye contact feels very bad mannered. Some people, even though it is an exercise, feel unable to do that part of it. The value of this exercise is to underline how we listen. Next time you are talking to someone, think about how they signal their ability to listen.

The Three Stage Listening Process

This process is about "actively listening". Try to resist questions since they can come from your agenda or opinions, and, as I have already indicated, they can divert someone away from the real issue.

Stage 1

When we are properly listening to someone we signal "I am with you" by using our:
* whole body
* facial expressions
* eye contact.

Stage 2

We encourage the person to talk by:
* remaining silent ourselves
* nodding, blinking our eyes
* making noises such as "Uh huh", "umm"
* using partial sentences such as "and ...", "go on ...", "so ...".

Stage 3

We help the person doing the talking to continue the story by:
* paraphrasing what they have said
* being genuinely empathic
* checking we've understood
* accepting the feelings that are expressed without judging
* checking we have picked up the correct feeling they are expressing
* using feeling centred questions such as:
    "How did that make you feel ..."
    "Your reaction to that was ..."
    "What would you like to do now ...".

A good listener does most of the above things.

* A good listener never gives advice unless specifically asked.
* A good listener tries never to be anecdotal about themselves, e.g.. "When I was your age ..." or "The exact same thing happened to me ..." I can almost guarantee your child will switch off.

Good quality listening will often lead to a person finding their own resolution to their problems. This is something counsellors find, it is also something parents discover when they start using it with their children. A good listener will hold and reveal certain attitudes and beliefs. Some of these are:

* listening is a facilitative process to enable a child (or adult) to find their own resolutions; a trust in the process of listening
* feelings can frequently be transitory.

The last point is important to remember. When you are deeply listening to a problem you will put a roadblock firmly into place if you start to say "but you didn't feel like that yesterday/last week". It is important to listen in a spirit of acceptance and without judgement. If your child is not able to resolve the problem for him or herself then you will keep the door open for you to go into problem solving, quite possibly at another time.

When serious listening is needed there are just a few more points to remember:

* try to have no interruptions such as television, other people, or the telephone
* do not expect to have the whole story in one go, you may need a lot of time
* this process takes as long as it takes - there is no time limit
* you have to be totally trustworthy.

As busy parents it is easy to encourage your child to talk to you when you are busy. Times like preparing the evening meal, cleaning the bathroom may be appropriate if you can do the job on "automatic pilot". This is particularly true if you are a family that has rarely communicated or made eye contact and find close physical proximity is uncomfortable. You can use stage two and three to good effect. Sometimes it is helpful to a child if they do not have the full weight of your anxious gaze. Recently a counsellor friend of mine was up to her elbows in ice, clearing out the freezer, when her eldest daughter approached her with a very difficult problem. She said that being partially engaged in something else seemed to help her daughter to talk. My friend did all the stage two and three responses while sorting the food in the freezer. With reflective responses from her mother the girl was able to resolve her problem herself.

As a general rule if your child needs to talk to you to explain a problem then you need to listen when you can give your full attention with your eyes, ears, body and mind. If you and your child have a regular time alone together it is likely that such time will be used to talk to you. If some private time is not available to your child then you will have to be aware if they are signalling to you that they need time to be made.

Parents Advice

Listening

1. Make a time when there are no interruptions. This is your time alone with your child.

2. Allow your child to talk without you interrupting with questions or advice.

3. Use the three stages of listening.

4. Ask if they wish for your comments.

5. Wait to be asked before offering advice.

6. Know what the roadblocks are.

Finally

1. Children will be childish because they are children.

2. Adults/Parents hold all the cards, parents are all-powerful.

3. Unless your child can read minds you need to tell your child how loved he/she is.

4. Children are the products of their upbringing.

5. If they live with love, they will know how to love.

6. If they live with cruelty, they will be cruel.

7. If the image you give them is poor, they will have a poor self-image.

Appendix 1

Autism

This group of children are becoming better known about in the general population. As babies they can be excessively passive or excessively distressed, and spend hours crying for no obvious reason. To be a parent of an autistic child is not easy.

With greater knowledge about autism more detailed diagnosis is possible and professionals talk about the autistic spectrum. They believe that there are degrees of autism and also a range of problems that give rise to similar symptoms. Children with autism share three common features:

* An inability to empathise. They have feelings of their own and can be hurt by others, but they will find it very difficult to understand other people's feelings.

* Communication and language difficulties. I still encounter children diagnosed with a receptive (understanding) and/or expressive language disorder and the nature of social difficulties has been missed. These children are more likely to be labelled antisocial than autistic. The whole area of communication is problematic, such as making appropriate eye contact and facial expressions in response to others' communication or as part of their own.

* Lack of imagination. They will be unlikely to understand humour. They need (and will create their own) routines, knowing what is to happen will be vital to their security. They are likely to be repetitive and obsessive in their movements and occupations.

Some autistic children will need specialist schooling whereas the majority who are described as being within the autistic spectrum will, with help, be managed in mainstream schools. They will always be perceived as odd or difficult in some way.

Appendix 2

Hyperactivity

This condition received a great deal of publicity in the 1980s. If one was to believe some press reports our schools were rapidly filling up with children with this problem to one degree or another. The causes of the problem are often speculated upon but the reality is that no one can really pin it down to one single thing. There is as much confusion about what causes it as by how to deal with it.

Professionals are in confusion and disagreement over causes, treatment and what to call it. The current favourite looks like Attention Deficit Disorder (ADD) or Attention Deficit Hyperactive Disorder (ADHD).

I believe the causes to be a mixture of a hereditary tendency, environmental factors (such as background pollution we all live with), diet, and the way some children are managed by their parents. The presenting hyperactivity can be due to one or all four.

Hyperactive or ADD children are every so often reported as noticeably active in the mother's womb. These children are then:

* often irritable, crying babies
* babies who rarely sleep
* need constant attention
* become very active as toddlers
* are much more likely than peers to touch, climb, etc. in a fearless way.

At school, teachers find them:

* inattentive
* disruptive
* clumsy and uncoordinated
* noisy
* fidgety
* easily distracted
* almost totally lacking in concentration
* having few friends.

One of the reasons that the ADHD label is useful in school is that it helps teachers to focus on the lack of attention and poor concentration rather than, as happened in the past, the focus being that of a naughty child.

Many ADHD children have a poor self-image that leads to low self-esteem. They sometimes have learning difficulties. Other children avoid them because they are so boisterous, pay little attention to boundaries, and are considered uncomfortable to be with.

What Can Be Done?

A truly hyperactive child is very rare. I have seen very few, in all the years I have worked with children with emotional and behavioural problems. There does however appear to be a continuum of difficulty, where a child may have only one or two problems through to the full range.

My first encounter with a child labelled hyperactive, some twenty years ago, was an American child who took a drug called Ritalin. We were horrified by what we believed to be the casual prescribing of a stimulant drug, whose long term effects on a child's brain were unknown. For the seriously hyperactive child it may be the only answer, or it may form a part of the answer.

In this country the Hyperactive Children's Support Group did much to get the condition researched. They also introduced the ideas of the late Dr Ben Feingold, who believed that food both natural foods and artificial additives were responsible for at least 50% of hyperactivity.

I was at the first conference he attended in this country to expound his theories. He was a warm, generous, caring man who was given a very rough time by the doctors present. Many parents were convinced that by taking their child off certain additives and foods their children calmed down. As a teacher I know I have seen an improvement in many children with various degrees of hyperactivity. As a parent I know the mood swings my own children are subject to if they overdose on certain drinks.

Unfortunately subsequent research into Feingold's theories has suggested an improvement in only a small number of children. I believe that these results suggest some fault in the research design is more likely, than that Feingold's theories could be so totally wrong.

The use of structured methods of handling children and definite behaviour modification programmes have some success with some children. It seems to me that the success of a programme is as dependent on the teacher or parent implementing it as on the child responding.

I would suggest that parents contact their doctors, who can recommend a dietician to help with an appropriate diet. The doctor can also refer the child to an occupational therapist who can do wonders for a clumsy and poorly co-ordinated child. The earlier both are started, the better.

When the child enters school the educational psychologist should be aware of any diagnosed hyperactivity, although in my experience it is not until a child enters school and is then expected to spend long periods sitting still and conforming that professionals start to look at the problem, even if the parents have been asking for help for years.

A way forward for older children that is having some success in America, and is beginning to be tried by some professionals here, is a three (sometimes four) pronged approach. The child is prescribed one of the amphetamine or related group of drugs such as Ritalin. These drugs have the effect of helping the child to focus more sharply, therefore concentrate and be considerably less fidgety. They become calmer and more accessible to teachers and friends.

Teachers and parents are given advice on how to manage the environment in a consistent and structured way as the second stage.

Finally, children are given individual counselling to help them understand why they are in this position, to help them focus on appropriate personal management strategies, and to feel better about themselves and their achievements.

For those children who also benefit in some way from diet therapy, this is not abandoned.

> *I can remember one mother saying to me that she had so much to thank the Hyperactive Children's support Group for. Her son was 14 years old. She remembered him as a difficult baby who was always crying. He was not cuddly, but cold and apparently angry. He ruined family occasions and never seemed happy. The diet really did help him.*

Bibliography

Bolton, R. (1987) People Skills : Australia, Simon and Schuster.

Bradshaw, J. (1991) The Homecoming, London, Judy Piatkus Publishing Ltd.

Bradshaw, J. (1993)Healing The Shame That Binds You Florida, Health Communications Inc.

Branden, N.(1992) The Power of Self Esteem: Florida, Health Communications Inc.

Davies, J., and Maliphant, R. (1974). quoted in Maines and Robinson(1991) Punishment, The Milder the Better. Bristol, Lucky Duck Publishing.

DES. (1989) Discipline in Schools. A report on the Committee of Enquiry, chaired by Lord Elton. London, H.M.S.O.

Dreikurs, R., Grey, L. (1970) A new approach to Discipline-Logical Consequences, Hawthorn Books, New York.

Dryden, G. and Vos, J. (1993) The Learning Revolution, Aylesbury, Bucks Accelerated Learning Systems.

Forward, S. (1989) Toxic Parents, New York, Bantum Books.

Gathorne-Hardy, J. (1977) The Public School Phenomenon, London, Hodder & Stoughton.

Ginot, H.G. (1956) Between Parent and Child, New York, Avon Books.

Graves, N.B. (1974) Inclusive Versus Exclusive Interaction Styles In Polynesian and European Classrooms, Research Report No.5. South Pacific Research Institute. Auckland. New Zealand.

Graves, N.B. and Graves, T.D. (1983) The Cultural Context of Prosocial Development: An Ecological Model in Bridgeman (Ed), The Nature of Prosocial Development: Interdisciplinary Theories and Strategies. New York Academic Press.

Gordon, T. (1976) Parent Effectiveness Training, New York, Perigee Books.

Lawrence, D. (1987) Self Esteem in the Classroom, London, Paul Chapman Publishing Limited.

Maines, B. and Robinson, G. (1991) Punishment the Milder the Better, Lucky Duck Publishing.

Maslow, A. (1954) Motivation and Personality, New York, Harper Row.

Maslow, A. (1962) Towards a Psychology of Being, London, Van Nastrand.

Mazlish, E. and Faber, A. (1974) Liberated Parents Liberated Children, New York, Avon Books.

Mazlish, E. and Faber, A. (1988) Siblings without Rivalry, London, Sidgewick & Jackson.

Miller, A. (1987:a) The Drama of being a Child, London, Virago.

Miller, A. (1987:b) For Your Own Good: Hidden Cruelty in Child Rearing and the Roots of Violence, London, Virago

Miller, A. (1991) Banished Knowledge, London, Virago.

Newell, P. (1989) Children are People Too, London, Bedford Square Press.

Rogers, C. (1969) Freedom to Learn, Ohio, Merrill.

Wright, A. (1990) Enhancing Motivation in Pupils and Adults, London, University College London Publications.

Resources and Contacts

Autism: Any book by Lorna Wing is very readable.

National Autistic Society,
276, Willesden Lane,
London,
NW2 5RB   Telephone 0181 451 1114

Hyperactive Children's Support Group (large SAE and stamp)
71 Whyke Lane,
Chichester,
West Sussex,
PO19 2LD

Attention Deficit Disorders Association (A5 SAE required for information)
P O Box 700,
Wolverhampton,
WV3 7YY

National Childbirth Trust
Alexandra House,
Oldham Terrace
London W3 6NH   Telephone 0181 992 8637